Relentless Love

First Sentient Publications edition, 2004

A paperback original.

Cover design by Kim Johansen, Black Dog Design
Book design by Nicholas Cummings


Library of Congress Cataloging-in-Publication Data

Smith, Edwin Carl, 1945-
  Relentless love : the power of a transformative life / Edwin Carl Smith.
     p. cm.
  ISBN 1-59181-021-3
  1. Love. I. Title.
BD436.S56 2004
177'.7--dc22

                                                            2004003958



Printed in the United States of America

10  9  8  7  6  5  4  3  2  1

## SENTIENT PUBLICATIONS

A Limited Liability Company
1113 Spruce St.
Boulder, CO 80302
www.sentientpublications.com

# Relentless Love

## The Power of a Transformative Life

### Edwin Carl Smith

SENTIENT PUBLICATIONS, LLC

Also by Edwin Carl Smith

DO YOU SEE WHAT I SEE?

# Contents

# About the Book

THIS BOOK IS ABOUT PERSONAL AND global transformation. It is therefore mythic in scope and language. You can become aware of, and so overcome, the mythic archetypes of thought, feeling, and experience that create your identity and organize your life by connecting the ideas in this book to personal life experiences. Otherwise, you can spend lifetimes overcoming the limitations of one unconscious archetypal thought before you are free of it enough to experience the ordinary enchantment of life.

Read this book for perception, not information. *Feel* what you read. Notice how you respond. Strong reactions are part of your liberation from archetypal patterns that create the drama of your life. Since the book is mythic and metaphoric, your experience of it will change as your life changes. Keep at it.

This book is about life when it is lived simply. Repeated reference to this book undermines the complexity of your life. What emerges is your natural genius and power to create and sustain an enchanted life in an enchanted land. So feel free to turn to pages at random. You may find deeper levels of meaning and possibilities for change when you do. Resort to it as you would any personal oracle.

Let all you read here turn all that you trust and believe into doubt and confusion. Why? Confusion signifies freedom and precedes all transformation. Freedom is the core of intelligence. Until your life trembles, you have no reason to trust anything but your present beliefs, experiences, and habits. Thus, enchantment eludes you. If you are already confused and in doubt, good! You will find here a reason and a way to reach out beyond confusion, to trust in the power and presence of your best intention, your most secret dream. When and if you begin to trust, your evolutionary journey will also begin.

To enchant your life, you will need an infinitely wise guide, more than this book certainly. That is the bad news. The good news is that such a guide is available to you in the form of your own life. You do not need spiritual practices, books, or great intellect. Your life is your guide and teacher. You need no other.

Enchantment means to live your life as a spiritual and mythic journey. Embrace life fully in all its dimensions. Do this and you will receive the full power and intelligence of life as a gift. You will awaken to a world enchanted by the presence and power of love.

Crossing the Line

There is a line that cannot be seen, but can be crossed.
It is the line that divides fiction from fact,
Creativity from madness,
The unknown from the known.
It separates your choices from your power.
It mocks your dreams, and ends your hopes.
It sucks your life dry and shrivels your soul.
The line is fear.
Beyond the line is a land you can imagine, but cannot see.
It is a land of possibility hidden from the world you call real.
It taunts you with what could be, and goads you with what is.
It is an initiation, a challenge, a test, a judgment.
I crossed that line. I live in the land of dreams.
It is a land of myth, and so a land of mystery.
It is a land of creative power, and so a land of magic and miracles.
It is a land of enchantment, and I am the enchanter.
I created the world of the enchanted earth: Ecos.
I created the archetypal path of the next age: Roar.
I created a life where dreams come true: the enchanter's game.
I created a new story beyond the end of this story.
Is this fantasy . . . or fact?
You are the judge. I am the witness.
What is your judgment?
There is an initiation, a doorway, a threshold, a line.
This is the line. Will you cross it?

# The Enchantment
# of Life on Earth

A TRANSFORMATIVE LIFE IS A TRANSFORMED life. Its power is the magical capacity to transform or enchant the world. Can human life ever be enchanted, magical, mythic, healing? The short answer is yes. The long answer is . . . this book. But the question seems premature. We are still asking if life can be good, moral, peaceful. Can we survive the next twenty years? Enchantment seems a long way off. But is it?

Mainstream religions have focused on making us good and moral. Esoteric spiritual traditions have focused on enlightenment—profound insight into our own true nature. Shamanic and pagan traditions focused on spiritual powers of various kinds. What if we could integrate all of these into a single possibility? What would we call it? *Enchantment*.

Enchantment is where your life and your dreams merge. It is that moment just ahead of your fear and learned cynicism. It is where life is fundamentally good, not because you are good but because life, the planet itself, is good, healing, nurturing, and supportive, not just as a metaphor, but in a literal and palpable way. Your job is not to interfere with it!

The key to enchantment is a secret our spiritual, religious, intellectual, and cultural traditions don't know or won't tell us. The core message of this book is considered secret in some traditions. In most traditions, it is not a secret—it does not have to be. It is trivialized as a dream of the past or future. The idea of enchantment has been with us a long time, as a distant memory of better times, as a hope for some utopian future. But let's cut to the chase and consider it as a pragmatic possibility now. After all, what do we gain by waiting? What do we lose by trying?

Enchantment is our nature in this life. We are natural wizards and enchanters with magical powers limited only by our imagination and skill. We have a natural capacity to enchant life on earth. Human life is already an inherently loving and wondrous play of health, freedom, power, and community. You must believe it before you can see it. You must see it before you can live it. You must live it before you can share it. You must share it to enchant the world, because enchantment demands to be shared. How is this possible? The answer is simple, but difficult to believe. You already know it. It is a test of your ability to suspend disbelief. The key to enchantment is . . . love.

Love is a learning and healing strategy of the body, not the intellect. It is not a simplistic romantic ideal. To love is to embrace the primordial energies of life itself. The result of a relentless love of life is evolution, the intelligent transformation of life: first you change inwardly, then you change outwardly, then you change the world.

## What Is Enlightenment?

Enlightenment is a term many people use and few understand. It is an event of deep personal change—the next step in your evolutionary journey. It is an important step, but it is only one step. We are all making that journey together, even if some move quickly ahead while others lag behind. Our evolution is not merely physical and personal. At its core, it is spiritual and impersonal, involving change in the organizing intelligence of life itself. The key to evolution, enlightenment, intelligence, enchantment—the key to our future for individuals and groups of every size and nature—is contained in a word that many use, few understand, and even fewer actually practice. That word is love.

I experienced enlightenment in 1975. I literally blundered my way into it, but that blunder served me well. It began a quest to understand enlightenment and how it happens. It is not what I thought it was. It probably is not what you think it is. And my quest led to a possibility beyond enlightenment: enchantment. Embedded in our humanity is a future in this world that exceeds our wildest dreams, but it can be achieved only by abandoning what we think we know or fear, especially about our future.

Enlightenment is easier to describe than to define. It is because enlightenment has no generally accepted definition that the term has its own mystique, shrouded in expectation and misinformation. I know that was true for me. A definition of enlightenment might be *a change of consciousness*, which is not very precise. It might be *a change of awareness within consciousness*, which is still not very informative. Enlightenment is difficult to define because it does not refer to a single experience or event. As you read personal descriptions, you realize there are many types, versions, and degrees of enlightenment. So, before I define enlightenment, let me first characterize its nature as I have come to understand it.

## Enlightenment Is Biased

Just as the speed of light is the only absolute in physics, so enlightenment is the only absolute among spiritual practitioners. And yet, every tradition has its own flavor of enlightenment. The details and metaphors used to describe or explain the event usually reflect personal, cultural, and religious history. It could be argued that this has more to do with the explanation than the actual event. True enough, but the context of an event influences its content. The experience of enlightenment varies among individuals and traditions. What people mean by enlightenment varies. What they experience varies. The results of the experience vary. Enlightenment, then, refers to a collection of events that result from a variety of personal changes in awareness, which vary with individual practice, purpose, and intention.

## Enlightenment Is Induced

Enlightenment may occur spontaneously, but it does not occur accidentally. Learning, for example, is a natural process, but what you learn is not. The exact moment you learn cannot be predicted and so it may appear to occur spontaneously, but it is without doubt part of a larger process. What you learn and how you learn reflect personal and cultural choices. Just so, enlightenment requires that your life be rooted in a singular intent—attention that relaxes fully into the body, where the intent is stored. It may be our collective evolutionary destiny, but enlightenment is a destiny we cannot assume will occur in spite of us. It must be chosen. Enlightenment is rooted in a natural process that must be engaged deliberately to achieve its fullest possibility beyond simple insight.

## Enlightenment Is Natural

So, enlightenment occurs spontaneously and intentionally. It is induced and natural. The process is so natural, in fact, it occurs immediately when you stop avoiding it. Of course, you must choose to stop avoiding it. This takes exception with the wisdom traditions, which use technical means to achieve enlightenment. Submitting to the body's evolutionary imperative, intent, and habit to love is the process of enlightenment. But I am getting ahead of myself.

The technical means (various forms of self-control, e.g., meditation) typically used to achieve enlightenment make it difficult to achieve, which explains why it takes so long. In other words, traditional means to enlightenment inhibit its natural underlying process. Traditional techniques only succeed when you succumb to this underlying natural bodily process, which usually occurs unnoticed and by accident. Thus, the real process of enlightenment remains a secret, even to those who experience it.

There is a natural and easeful process at the root of enlightenment. You could infer then that the arbitrary and unnecessary technical means to enlightenment used by the traditions serve another purpose, or reflect a failure to comprehend the real process at the root of enlightenment, or both.

## Enlightenment Is Not an Insight

It is becoming common to distinguish traditional enlightenment from evolutionary enlightenment. I will honor that distinction. Traditional enlightenment involves an insight that reveals your original face, your nature prior to form in any dimension. But this does not mean what you might think it does. Enlightenment reveals your true nature—and that is all! It is an insight, nothing more. That is enough for most people apparently. So, teaching typically follows enlightenment. What else can you do with an insight, after all? The master clings to the insight, but not to the freedom or power that made it possible. That would require putting your life at risk, literally—yielding to the raw power of life, living unselfconsciously, without control or defense, vulnerable to the vagaries of spirit.

To live freely before one has had the insight of freedom—to succumb utterly to spirit, the body, and the demands of an ordinary infinite life without creating chaos for others—is a journey most people do not take. Why? You cannot end the journey by getting up from your meditation cushion. To live fully and freely in life, put yourself at its mercy. Allow the primordial energy of life to live you.

If you do that, the result is more than great insights and a life spent teaching about the joys of liberation. You go from beginner's mind to a permanent beginner's life. You are always living ahead of the comfortable familiarity of your insights. You encounter life before your insights kick in. This is a truly and literally humbling life, and the essence of freedom. It grounds you. But it begs the question "Now what?" After liberation, what do you do? The traditional answer is to take up the literal details of life: washing the dishes, mowing the lawn. We must do these things to live our life, but it completely misses the larger possibility of living life in the moment before enlightenment itself.

## You Must Sacrifice Enlightenment

Your original face is not a personal identity, but life itself. Through insight you understand that your true identity is no-identity. But to live freely, you must first transcend personal identity by surrendering awareness into the formless Primordial Spirit. Then you must sacrifice that freedom from personal identity to the demands of ordinary life. The result is enchantment, ordinary life without boundaries, an ordinary infinite life. Freedom is a necessary pre-condition to enchantment, but it must inform your life. It cannot *be* your life. Those who try to live freedom literally, create chaos around them. There is no compassion in such crazy wisdom. There is no compassion in freedom or enlightenment.

When the self disappears into the utter emptiness and freedom of life, you discover there is nobody home to live your life. So, after the event of enlightenment, you must choose one of three options: 1) assume a traditional or conventional role or identity, 2) live without a role or identity (i.e., in chaos), or 3) transcend (live ahead of) enlightenment to create a role or identity. In other words, enlightenment cannot tell you how to live an ordinary, infinite, enchanted life!

## You Must Sacrifice Freedom

You have no freedom of action in this life. You only have the freedom of intelligence, which is not freedom as most people understand it. You are always free to act arbitrarily and without intelligence, of course, but not without consequence. That is not freedom. Thus, a life without the limiting and controlling influence of intelligence can only be a life of struggle. To end the struggle, you must jump ahead of actions, thought, feeling, and personal and collective belief. You must get out of your mind and encounter your body's intelligence directly. Only there can you have any freedom. After that moment, the game of life is fixed. Your life is the inescapable drama of your life intelligence.

To live freely, you must align yourself with the intelligence or energetic intent of the body, which is love. Love is the body's only intent. It is that implicit intent or habit that connects us to life. Thus, love is the only life intent any of us can have, or we suffer. We set up a conflict with our selves and life generally, which is not the definition of freedom.

Once you are consciously aligned with your body's intent to love, you are free to live any purpose in life consistent with love. Purpose, which generates personal identity and social role, is a self-imposed limit on your infinite possibilities. Thus, your experience of life depends on freedom from conflict with the intent to love and a life purpose congruent with love. Your identity or role in life is not a given or a choice. It is a creation.

Freedom is necessary for life, but it cannot be lived in life. Freedom from everything leaves you in a void and you cannot experience a void. There is nothing to experience! Where's the fun of that? Human life can only occur in the context of limits.

The freedom you seek and need is freedom from the limits imposed by fear. Fear limits your capacity to give and receive love—the energy and intelligence of life and the energetic intent of the body. Enlightenment frees you from the stupidity of fear. But then, since you can, you must live without fear, in courage, in love. You must embrace life, not retreat from it. But who or what purpose will you serve in life? Enlightenment cannot answer that question. The answer is in the moment before enlightenment.

## Enlightenment Is a Political Event

Enlightenment changes your inner life, but not your outer life. So, traditions offer a culturally defined outer life or role as a solution. But that contains, rather than expresses, the intelligence of life that only enlightenment can liberate. Your liberation is then a personal and private attribute with no impact on the community or tradition. That is why they offer such a role, to avoid the impact of intelligence, the demand for love. Enlightenment has political and social consequences on a global scale, unless we prevent it by succumbing to the traditional promise of social acceptance. But to succumb to the intelligence of life that enlightenment liberates, you must have the courage to live in the moment before any wisdom appears. And you must embrace life outside the context of socially defined roles.

## Enlightenment Is the Way to Life

Enlightenment is not the pinnacle of spirituality. It is an important beginning in a much larger process. First, you must transcend reality in all its dimensions. Then you must embrace it in all its dimensions. Finally, you must transform it in all its dimensions. Transcend your self, embrace your life, transform your world and ultimately, human experience. If you do not pursue this possibility, you prevent the world from evolving.

## Freedom Without Power Is a Waste

Freedom from the limits of life and wisdom about this life must have power, or what is it for? Until we are free of who we have been individually, we cannot create who we can be collectively. We cannot know who we can be. The purpose of freedom and enlightenment is not to be free of the past, but to be free to create a future in this life that is not rooted in the past. Thus, there cannot be a traditional identity or role to express enlightenment. Any such thing is a fraud, a benighted response to the opportunity of enlightenment. There can be no traditional response to the power and intelligence of life. The only legitimate and honest response is personal creativity. But what do you create? Who shall you be, now that you are nothing? Enlightenment has no answer. It opens the door in silence to an opportunity ahead of itself. If you take that opportunity, you leap ahead of the traditions. Then you must find and create a path back to ordinary life that does not capitulate to its history. But how, and for what purpose?

## Ordinary Life Is Not Small

Freedom is a waste if you only talk about it. Freedom has no meaning or purpose when you retreat into the literal smallness of life. The ability to live ordinary life on an infinite scale is available only in the moment before enlightenment (but after the event), when ordinary and mythic mean the same thing.

Freedom is the context of all intelligent change. But the purpose of freedom is not personal. Rather, personal freedom must be sacrificed in the fires of an ordinary infinite life, which will, to be sure, demand more of you than washing dishes and mowing the lawn. In the moment before enlightenment, the body's intent to love interacts with others on a global scale—a direct transformation of life on a global scale. This is the possibility of enchantment. It is not and cannot be the result of traditional enlightenment.

## Enchantment Is a Creation, Not a Tradition

That there has been no global transformation during the centuries that people have experienced enlightenment says something about the traditions and their practitioners. Their agenda is to avoid personal power. Those people whom we agree really did change the world did not avoid power; they embraced it. They were not exceptional people; they just made an exceptional choice and the result of that choice was exceptional. Imagine a world of such people. Traditional enlightenment reveals an inherent bias: freedom from this world and life, freedom from the power to live creatively in all dimensions. The traditions resist the possibility that only enlightenment makes possible.

## Reality as Five Realms

Let me take a moment to clarify some concepts. Imagine reality as five realms: the physical, the personal (mind and emotions), the mythic, the intentional, and the energetic. These realms are nested one within the other in the order given, except for the energetic realm, which suffuses all the others. All realms connect to and influence each other.

That is the metaphysical model of reality we will use. Interestingly, each realm has an analog in the human body. There is enough research on brain functions to associate this metaphysical model with specific brain structures, but for the sake of clarity, let's not insist on too much accuracy. The brain consists of three structures: the neo-cortex, the mid-brain, and the brainstem. The physical realm refers to the body as a whole. The personal realm refers to the neo-cortex—self-awareness, intellect, your sense of self. This is the thinking self. Emotions tend to emanate from the mid-brain (a.k.a. the limbic system or mammalian brain), but can be influenced by activity of the thinking self. The mythic realm consists of organizing archetypes—energetic patterns that structure our experience of reality. Its analog is the interaction of the mid-brain and the brainstem. The intentional realm has its analog in the brainstem. The brainstem and the mid-brain are the two oldest parts of the brain. Taken together, they form the Original Self. The energetic realm permeates the other realms and animates them all.

## The Limits of Freedom

Practitioners of mystic traditions are taught to ignore all realms but the energetic—the Source, the realm of complete freedom, where all things are born and die. Clearly, it is not possible to embrace the fullness of ordinary life when you train yourself to focus on the formless freedom of pure energy and ignore everything else. One reason traditions arise is to respond to this self-imposed limitation. Since esoteric traditions are generally uninterested in the enlightenment or enchantment of ordinary life, and since they offer no real help in living such a life, ways must be found to support those who master and fulfill the possibilities of the tradition. Thus, masters generally keep their lives within a tradition, safe from the unsettling demands of enchantment, free from the demands of responsibly managing ordinary life in the context of infinite power and intelligence.

## Traditional Enlightenment Has an Agenda

Traditional enlightenment satisfies an implicit desire to end the travails of embodied life. The desire to avoid reincarnation stems from a fear of life and is exemplified in the misinterpretation of the Buddha's insight that life is clouded with suffering and struggling. This insight does not imply that suffering and struggling are inherent in life, only that they are our experience in life. To assume life causes our experience is inherently disempowering. To assume that we cause our experience makes it possible to end human suffering in this world rather than escape it. We can enchant life on earth!

## Meditation Generates Unawareness

Let us turn briefly to the core technology of enlightenment: meditation. Traditional meditation practices have one thing in common: focused attention. There are so many ways to focus, manipulate, structure, manage, and alter attention that we take focused attention for granted. But focused attention is a better definition of concentration than meditation, or there is no difference between them. To focus attention on anything restricts awareness of everything else. In other words, meditation generates unawareness.

Traditional meditation results in self-imposed limitation, because method controls outcome and makes it predictable. If our methods did not generate predictable results, we would stop using them. The purpose of method and technique, then, is control. So, can freedom result from methods that control, limit, and exclude? The short answer is no. The long answer is that meditation witnesses freedom, but only within a field so narrow it excludes embodied life! Meditation expresses and reinforces the problem of human life—our separation from life and our resulting inability to love. Meditation disempowers us by disconnecting us from our body, from the body's capacity to love, from life. It elevates the obstacles to life to the level of worship. Thus, enlightenment (the fruit of meditation) cannot solve the problem (overcome the limits) of ordinary life. It is the problem.

Ordinary life has no inherent limits or barriers. Yet enlightened masters live as though the conditions of life are a given and freedom is only a personal experience. In a world without barriers, one person's liberation frees the world—the whole of reality actually—unless that person retreats from the possibility of enchanting ordinary life.

## Tradition Is the Death of Enchantment

Traditions largely agree with the common and unexamined premise that life sucks. Enlightenment reveals complete freedom beyond embodied life. This would seem to prove freedom is elsewhere, not in the body anyway, and so cannot be lived in this life. But the traditions create a result that justifies their premise. Enlightenment is the goal of those who wish to avoid ordinary life rather than enchant it. Not only does the method control the outcome, the method *is* the outcome. You create what you practice. If you practice exclusion, you achieve it. If you narrow attention, you create unawareness. The traditions cannot generate freedom in this life. Their premise excludes the possibility.

The mythic promise of enlightenment—peace and freedom—is not and cannot be its outcome, at least not in this world. Enlightenment reflects a preference for mind over body. Enlightenment is not about the power and wisdom of the body, which is love. Yet life is the embodiment of power and energy. So what is enlightenment and what good is it?

## What Is Enlightenment?

Enlightenment is the reorganization of awareness around a single purpose. This means that enlightenment varies with purpose. When awareness is organized around a single purpose you have a natural inclination to insight and wisdom that we call genius. Enlightenment occurs when your purpose is spiritual, when attention is focused on whatever that means to you. Enchantment—the final expression and fulfillment of evolution before it moves beyond individuality into community—requires that your personal purpose be congruent with the body's intent or habit of love.

The power of personal purpose and intent is well known to shamans, but you find little or no reference to it in the wisdom literature. Why? Because if purpose controls experience and enlightenment (which it does), then we live in a much different world than we thought, and enlightenment is less than we hoped. We live in a world of wizards. To be embodied is to have magical powers. That power is managed by purpose, not wisdom. The scope of your freedom exceeds the scope of any enlightenment. The difference is managed by personal purpose. Purpose is the root of enlightenment, not meditation.

## Enlightenment Is a Franchise

Practitioners and partisans may not notice the purpose embedded in the fabric of every culture, tradition, and practice. Purpose need not be conscious to be active. The variety of experiences suggests that enlightenment does not transcend purpose but is induced by it, and that every tradition franchises their version of enlightenment.

Traditions offer a franchised reality in which we live. Reality is a cultural purpose imposed on personal experience through the force of tradition. When you practice a tradition, you practice the purpose of that tradition. So, within a tradition, enlightenment always appears transcendent because its purpose remains unnoticed.

Accounts by those who achieve enlightenment make it clear they have no idea what causes it. Most accounts offer statements within a tradition revealing no particular insight into the process. From inside a tradition, you cannot tell if enlightenment results from your practice or something else. A practice is a specific way to engage the natural process of life, but awareness of that underlying process usually gets lost in your focus on the practice and its goal. Thus, the traditions franchise a natural process freely and directly available to anyone since it is embedded in your own body.

The politically correct way to address this issue is to say that all paths lead to the same destination. Of course, no one really believes that. If they did, there would be no partisans. We would all be living in happy togetherness. Traditions would not matter. But they do matter to those in them. Why? Because traditions embody different purposes, employ different practices to manifest those purposes, achieve different goals, and promote different experiences. All of this is done using a common process at the creative core of human experience. This makes it clear that the differences between traditions are superficial, irrelevant, imposed, and purposeful. Spiritual traditions are personal fashion, not truth.

## Enlightenment Is the Root of Genius

Enlightenment organizes awareness around a single purpose, but what purpose? Enlightened masters are like college graduates. The degree is nice but the real issue is their major. Traditional enlightened masters majored in what? Their tradition, of course. And that is the problem. Traditions are artifacts of human ingenuity and creativity. Further, they express the creative choices of our past. They offer no clue to our future. Indeed, all traditions territorialize human experience and then franchise their vision of our possibility. That was then, this is now. What is our future? We must choose, individually and collectively. We created our past. We can and must create our future.

## Humanity Is Joined by Its Creativity

Every action, thought, and feeling—everything we do at every level—betrays a purpose. Choosing our purpose is our first and only true creative act. Ordinary life just elaborates our purpose. We manage the power embedded in life through purpose. Human life is not a given. It is not something to which we must adapt. It is rather an energetic system for manifesting our purpose, our dreams. Human experience is an illusion not because it is not real, but because it is something we create. We can recognize our humanity in the equality of our creative power and in the diversity of our creations.

## The Future of Enlightenment

We must expand our definition of enlightenment or fall prey to the limits and failures of our traditions. First, if freedom is to have any meaning for us, it must include life in all dimensions. The idea that the body, for instance, is a limitation and therefore antithetical to freedom is untrue and the result of limited awareness. The body is not a limit on the infinite. It offers access to the infinite in every dimension, something unavailable in every other dimension of life. The higher realms are not freer than the lower realms, just the reverse. The limitation of the higher realms is the absence of physical form. Only in embodied form do we have access to the whole of the created and uncreated realms.

## Things We Cannot Avoid

We cannot avoid life. The body is a relentless embrace of life. We can only give in to its natural inclination to love or suffer the result.

We cannot avoid power. Life is the drama of our use or misuse of power. Either way, we cannot avoid it. We can only learn to use it intelligently or suffer the result.

We cannot avoid love. Love is also a risk, but it is a risk our bodies are already taking for us. Love is the only context for a humane life without inherent barriers, a life worth living, safe from making the future an extension of our past, free of the scourge of fear.

We cannot avoid purpose. Experience is organized around our purpose, encoded energetically in the body. Since we are unaware of this, we think we experience reality.

We cannot avoid life, love, power, and purpose, yet these define our struggles.

To be alive is to live in all dimensions. To live in enchantment is to live in all dimensions without barriers. Embodied life enables us to live on an infinite scale. The question is what will we do with our power? To answer that question responsibly, we must be free of the past, or we will only find new ways to repeat it. But that alone is not enough to create a future beyond our individual and collective history. That demands a recognition of and surrender into our personal and collective intent to love. Only from there can we manage our power. Only there will the future be safe from the past and any new form of unconsciously imposed limits. And only there is the perennial conflict between personal power and global community resolved.

Enlightenment is the organization of awareness around a single purpose. Enchantment is the organization of life around the single and unavoidable bodily intent to embrace life in all dimensions. We can and must align the purpose of the thinking self with the intent of the Original Self. Only then will personal evolution and the promise of enlightenment fulfill their destiny. Only then will life be more than a goad to escape it, or to limit our experience of it. Only then will ordinary life transcend all barriers to love. Only then will ordinary life be the mechanism and context for personal and collective greatness.

## Love Is Our Natural Spiritual Strategy and Path

Human experience is the result of the play between purpose and intent. It is clear that to optimize our experience of life, our purpose must align with the body's intent to love. If we define love as the courage to embrace life and each other without barriers or boundaries, we create the conditions for enlightenment on a global scale.

Life is lived best when it is lived most simply, in love. This has profound implications for personal and collective spiritual practice and the enchantment of life on earth.

# The Crucible of Love

My first enlightenment came at the very beginning of my path, in my conversion. There was an immediate revelation, a perceptual shift that opened the door to a vision of a natural spiritual path embedded in ordinary life. The thinking self made it its purpose to trust the wisdom of the body, the Original Self. As the mind relaxed into the body, there was a revelation. Evolution occurs as brain functions reorganize and integrate.

My second enlightenment, which was of the mind and the personal realm, came about five years later. My mind was transformed, permanently altered. The landscape of my inner life shifted. My conversion to love had resulted in a permanent restructuring of self-awareness. The functions of the thinking self reorganized and optimized, resulting in enlightenment.

My third enlightenment, which was of the heart and the mythic realm, occurred six months later. In that moment I died (self-awareness disappeared) and was reborn (identity organized itself into a new pattern). It sounds dramatic, but at the time it was just another experience. It did not take long, however, to realize the world around me had changed. I saw the world everyone else sees, but I also saw it in its moment of origin, in its fullness, before we try to improve it. I wrote a book about it. The connection between the neo-cortex and the mid-brain, which primarily handles root emotions, reorganized. The mid-brain contains basic energetic habits to filter incoming life information and organize it into experiences congruent with your purpose.

My fourth enlightenment, which is of the body and the intentional realm, continues. The changes seem kinder, smaller, more numerous, less muscular, but no less powerful. It took a while to realize that love was moving out into the world—testing, probing for those willing to take up the challenge of life in the transforming crucible of love. The energy moved in subtle ways, changing possibilities rather than events, in my life and in the lives of others. I looked down the path it was creating. I saw the enchantment of life on earth. When this occurs, brainstem functions are optimizing and integrating with other brain structures and the body generally. The energy of evolution moves through the body into the world.

So ends the natural spiritual path of individuality. And so begins the next evolutionary phase, the Enchanter's Game, the magical play of individual creativity in the context of enlightened community.

## The Way of Love

What do we actually do when we love? To love is to embrace life and each other in complete trust, to be able to receive and to give the blessings of life. To love, you must be available to the raw, primordial power of life. The ancient word for this power is spirit—the free, unformed, untamed energy of life. This energy flows through the body and life generally as a constant and unavoidable source of joy, health, and creative power. As you relax, become silent, turn from the distractions of ordinary life and make yourself consciously available to life, you will notice this flowing energy. To relax into and merge with the power of life is to love and to be loved. It generates deep change. It is not a romantic ideal. Love is transforming because it connects you directly to the power of life. It is not to be approached casually. It will not improve your life. It is disruptive, messy, demanding, and uncompromising. While people say they want love, not everyone tolerates the transforming results of being loved by life.

## The Spiritual Establishment

Spirituality is in vogue. Enlightenment is cool. But the transforming power of life is trivialized and lost when it goes mainstream. A tragic air surrounds spiritual endeavors. When you pursue what you do not expect to achieve and are unprepared to accept, the result can only be tragic. Such ambiguity, if not hypocrisy, is unworthy of us. It trivializes our future and makes the enchantment of life on earth just another phrase to market.

Spiritual practitioners and teachers often fumble in a darkness of good intentions. Enlightenment is so unpredictable, practitioners are instructed not to make it a goal of their practice! Generally it is regarded as a theoretical possibility at best. Practices are meant to help you become a good member of a tradition, not enlightened. Such practices do not prevent enlightenment, but they are no inducement either.

## New Wine, Old Skins

Spiritual and religious traditions are franchises that offer experiences and lifestyles for sale. Spiritual and religious experiences are generated by resort to proprietary beliefs and practices that implement a specific cultural purpose, each religion developing its niche in the global marketplace. This is not a bad thing. It is in fact the wave of the future: pick your game, choose your reality. But these experiences, beliefs, practices, are certainly not the truth. The truth that creates and organizes your reality is a personal choice, not a given truth to which all must submit. Life is a game to be sure, and we are free to pick the game of life we want to play, the experience of life we want to have. But let us play the game on purpose, not by accident, with skill and grace—not ineptness, narcissism, fear and partisanship, which is adolescent.

Life is very much like a global theme park. It is fun to enjoy our days at the park, but sooner or later we must account for our impact on it. We must take responsibility for maintaining the park at the very least. Ultimately, we must create new attractions, new forms of experiences, clean up the trash, and get rid of what no longer works. We cannot be simply tourists in our own life and world.

Evolving from consumer to creator demands a higher order of life intelligence, not religious beliefs and practices. Traditions franchise experiential themes in the global park of life. Our responsibility is not to themes or history, but to the park itself.

The question now is should we choose any of the existing experiential franchises? To fulfill our human responsibility and destiny as enchanters of life, we must recognize the inherent bias of all traditions against that which we most value: intelligence, creativity, power, love, community, health. We must forego our parochial allegiances to culture, belief, tradition, worldview, or personal identity. If we are to solve the problems we face, we must evolve beyond our limited view of what is real and true. But even that is only prelude to a higher level of life intelligence that will afford us the skills to solve our current problems and create still undreamed possibilities. We can no longer solve our problems by improving our life. We must transform our life and world, intelligently. Changing religious affiliations, personal preferences, or lifestyle will not solve any personal, let alone global, problem. If we are not to drown in the waste of irresponsibility and immaturity, we must express a higher form of human intelligence, and build a world around it. That form of human intelligence is love.

## Personal and Global Evolutionary Intelligence

The archetypal metaphor of evolution is death. Reorganizing awareness ends your life and world as you have known them. The popularity of mystical and pagan practices is a mixed blessing. As we amuse ourselves with spiritual experiences or insights, we prolong our adolescence by refusing the call to maturity. The eternal child archetype must be a personal quality, not an identity.

Even though life is interactive play, death is still the backstage door to the creative process behind what we call reality. We are, right now, magicians of life—inept magicians to be sure because we do not yet realize our power, but no less powerful for our lack of skill. We do not take responsibility for our play of life because we think we are only consumers. We suffer the delusion that the play of life is created elsewhere. The result of centuries of such intelligence is all around us.

Evolution is deep change, altering the root of experience and reality itself. It will not fit in your hip pocket. It is not convenient, something to practice at your leisure when you want to get centered. To be fully alive is to be gloriously overwhelmed by life's possibilities. For you to evolve, life must overwhelm you.

## The End of Childhood

Not many people are free. Most are partial to a truth or belief, a franchised story of life. All such stories limit your freedom. Each truth is a temporary convenience that thwarts intelligence. Life calls us to greater love, more learning, greater flexibility. We cannot do that in the context of old habits of mind and heart. We must evolve.

Traditional spiritual and religious practices and paths focus on proper or true beliefs because they are more concerned with perfection than learning. Are you afraid to make mistakes? A truly spiritual life is not about fear. It is about the joy of living, being unafraid of mistakes.

Hear then, the call to personal and collective evolutionary intelligence and destiny—a call to the end of childhood and adolescence, a call to evolve so human life is a glory and a joy, not a trial and a trauma. What follows is a fearless strategy for living ordinary life that results in evolutionary intelligence.

Row, row, row your boat
Gently down the stream.
Merrily, merrily, merrily, merrily,
Life is but a dream.
OR
Live your life gently
As in a flowing stream.
Merrily, joyfully, luckily—or not,
You are living a dream.

# On the Threshold
# of Love

## Evolutionary Learning

PHYSICALLY, HUMAN BEINGS SEEM TO EVOLVE from conception to birth. Then we mature until the moment of death. But we exist in five realms. The evolutionary imperative continues after birth. It moves us consciously from one realm to the next, unless we prevent it. Interestingly, it is not an evolution of external form but of internal function.

Our mental and emotional, or personal, evolution proceeds to adolescence (formal thought), then it seems to stop. Why? Modern cultures work to extend adolescence, to forestall the next evolutionary phase of human intelligence and maturity, by emphasizing mental intelligence over emotional intelligence, inhibiting the natural tendency of the body to optimize the connection between the neo-cortex and the mid-brain.

Some of us are active in the mythic realm through affiliations with religious or other spiritual endeavors, but learning there is mostly adolescent as well. By focusing on what to believe (thinking self) rather than how to perceive (Original Self), we substitute collective orthodoxy for personal integrity. Worse, our mythic-level beliefs disavow personal power, yet the mythic realm is all about the energetic or empowered connection between thought and matter. Our local and global myths of democracy, for instance, are all interpreted to make it impolitic to explore possibilities at this level. After all, if we were all free and empowered beings, would we need representative democracy?

Few people function consciously in the intentional realm. There are no traditional paths to this realm, though some traditions do mention it exists.

The energetic realm is the raw energy of life, vibrating, pulsating, roaring in all things. Nothing and no one exists here, since it is unorganized energy, but without it, nothing could exist or change.

We are familiar with the physical and personal realms, but we also exist in the mythic and intentional realms. Contemporary life is a challenge to continual adolescence. Now, we must manage our myths and the purpose for creating them. We are at the natural end of evolution in the physical and personal realms. We are now creating problems we cannot solve until we embrace a higher evolutionary level.

## The Two Selves

How can this be done? Let us start at the beginning: to enchant life on earth, you must do something silly but quite powerful in its impact. You must trust that you exist! Let me explain.

The thinking self must trust the original self. What? Well, the original self consists of the two most ancient parts of our brain. It is where we perceive reality (rather than think about it). The original self cannot block out life's energy. It is directly connected to and indistinguishable from reality. For all practical purposes, it is reality. The original self is in a constant mystic union with all realms, at once. Indeed, when we are fully engaged with life through the original self, self-awareness (the thinking self), disappears. As the thinking self relaxes, the functional barriers between brain structures that form our sense of self also relax. The thinking self begins getting life information from the original self before self-awareness forms. The thinking self experiences this information as intuition.

Living only as a thinking self cannot be done, but we try, and that sets up a conflict between brain functions that prevents evolutionary intelligence. So how do we integrate the Thinking and Original selves? Try love. Now we come to trusting yourself.

Presume that you exist prior to self-awareness as the original self. This is literally true. The information processing functions of the brainstem and mid-brain all occur before you are self-aware. Presume that love is the nature of your original self. To do otherwise creates a functional barrier in the brain to your capacity to give and receive love. The presumption that you exist prior to self-awareness as love aligns the thinking self with the natural functions of the original self. Now trust your body, your original self: embrace life and experience it as love. The presumption of love and your continuing act of trust shifts the context of your experience of life. The result is enchantment.

Love on earth is created by an initial act of courage (self-trust) and fulfilled by continuing acts of faith. The journey from here to enchantment is rooted in a simple strategy that optimizes the body's own natural process. It is so simple it is not quite believable. It takes a book to explain (even a bit) what can be stated in a sentence. It takes a life to explore the depth of that possibility.

## Evolutionary Crisis
Evolutionary learning is a prolonged identity crisis. Everything you recognize as you is a limitation to be overcome. The thinking self overcomes its limits by trusting the original self, and so be connected to life in that moment before it is aware, before it can think, or know anything at all. You must embrace life before you can notice you are doing it! How? Presume love. Act on that presumption (i.e., trust). Then notice what happens. So, your purpose is now aligned to your body's intent to love. Watch out!

## The Genius of Not Knowing
Not knowing is the basis for learning. Intelligence is all about not knowing. When you presume not-knowing, then trust, your body opens and fills with the intelligence of love. Such evolutionary learning is the alternative to struggling with life.

Evolutionary learning does not focus on knowledge. Knowledge is a byproduct of evolution, not its purpose. If you can learn by practicing ignorance and trusting your original self, you don't need to know anything to live an enchanted life. You learn without needing to remember what you learn because your life is rooted in what you perceive now, not what you remember. In ignorance you have access to all the knowledge on earth. You are a genius, not because of what you know, but because you can perceive.

The key to fulfilling our dreams of enlightenment, evolution, community, whatever, is simpler than you imagine. Just relax, and your dreams will come true. It is nothing esoteric. We can fill many books, like this one, with meaningful and important ideas about transforming our lives and our world, but it all comes down to the simplicity of a single word like relax, or trust, or faith, or love. It is nothing cognitive. There is nothing to know, only something to do: relax, trust, have faith, love. Pick one and live it.

# Living Ahead of Your Mind

The strongest influence on our thoughts and perceptions is culture. Cultures socialize us, teach us what to notice, what to value, what to befriend, fear, think, feel. Socialization is mass hypnosis. Our experiences occur inside a culturally induced trance. Cultures are deliberate deceptions. They do not help us perceive reality. They induce a consensus experience about reality.

To be sure, socialization is not entirely effective or no one could awaken from the trance. But it is enough to maintain social order. It is more effective than we like to admit, especially in cultures that value individuality and self-responsibility. Try to notice the influence of culture on every aspect of your life.

## The Limiting Influence of Culture

Societies do not want intelligent, free, empowered, creative people in their midst. Such people are troublesome, unpredictable. Societies want hard-working, docile, and orderly citizens to promote the social good (purpose). So societies franchise a worldview of powerlessness through religious and social institutions. We take socialization for granted because it is everywhere. Worse, we believe it. We view life from inside the prison of our socialized mind. We identify with our culture (its purpose) without question. We are extensions of our culture, living out its gloomy vision.

But as problematic as all of this may be to our human destiny, we would be much worse off without it! The problem is that we internalize our culturally induced reality. We do not consider that our reality might not be the only, let alone the best, reality. All other possibilities are suspicious. They are foreign. Of course, there is no best reality. Our goal is not to find the best or right reality, but to free ourselves from all of them because they are all self-induced, arbitrary fictions. Only then can we create, alter, and move among realities to create a fiction of choice and enjoy the play of life.

## The Matrix of Your Mind

The original self perceives reality directly. But the thinking self projects an image onto the stage of life that you regard as you. You bypass the original self (your only direct connection to life) because you consider only the image of you as real.

Reality is a vast and empty field of energy—a theater. You are the theater, not the play. Once you think the play (the image of you in a world of images) is real and limit your awareness to that image, you are powerless because the image of you is only a powerless image of the real you, the original self. You are trapped in the matrix of your mind. Your mind is your prison until you free it. But who will free you?

Sometimes our personal dramas do not fit within our culture's purpose. If not, we can 1) succumb to the play (domestication); 2) resist the play (rebellion); 3) understand what creates the play and opt out, claiming it is all illusion (insight); or 4) create a better play (enchantment). What are you choosing?

## Your Life Is Your Play

So, the cultural play limits awareness. That is how it becomes reality. We limit our awareness to the play of life, to the effect rather than the cause. We forget we are the cause and not just the effect. We cannot wake up to end or alter our participation in the play. We lose control of our life. The awakening of enlightenment reminds us we are not merely actors in a cosmic play, we are creators. Without awakening, we experience only personal delusion: unawareness, alienation, separation, anxiety, fear, and ignorance.

We limit our awareness to the images created by the thinking self. Life occurs outside that field of awareness, and affects us, but we are unaware of it. So, we often cannot account for our experiences. We respond with fear, withdrawal, or anger, or perhaps we try to control our life. Our choices are limited by our limited awareness of our true situation. There is no escape from this handicap save awakening from the arbitrary nature of reality. But that is only a beginning. Awakening is not living. You must go beyond enlightenment to enchantment, where you consciously connect to and embody the full power of life. But that is still insufficient for an enchanted life. You must express the power of your enchantment on earth. It all begins with the presumption of love. This is the secret of evolution and the key to living as an enchanter in an enchanted land.

### The Limits of Knowledge

Cultures train us to be true believers. We see what we believe. We trust what we believe. We live what we believe. This is great for social stability, not for evolution. Belief and faith are not opposed, but the broader awareness that comes from trusting life before belief gives you access to more information, as well as power, wisdom, and deep community. There is more to perceive of life than we believe.

The choice to love is made by the thinking self and lived by the original self. The thinking self depends on the original self to experience the enchantment of life. For that, you must relax.

### The Limits and Power of Thoughts

Thoughts do not and cannot create experience unless they are empowered, connected to the body. For that you must presume love and trust the original self, which is the creator of experience. Thus, thoughts have the power to manifest as experience when we trust the original self—our connection to the power and natural enchantment of life.

So now we have a way to understand personal experience. The original self is our true intent to love. The thinking self experiences the play created by the interaction of its purpose with the intent of the original self. So far so good, but any purpose other than love interferes with the natural play of life. Therein is the complication that generates the dilemma of ordinary life and makes life distinctly unloving.

The thinking self functions independently of real life, which is both a strength and danger. When the selves are congruent, experience is good. When they are not, experience is bad. We ensure congruence by connecting the two selves and making the thinking self secondary to the original self. Trust connects the two selves and makes the original self primary. Relaxation is the physical expression of trust.

## The Coming of Enchantment

There is only one reality, but we experience reality intuitively, and our ideas about reality consciously. Our brain generates two views of reality, but we are aware of only one—the world of images and the story that explains and justifies them. But we are not our story, our history, or our experiences.

When you limit awareness to the thinking self, you lose the informational input from the original self. The energy of life affects you, but unconsciously, and you react to this invisible influence as something unknown and not to be trusted or loved. You cannot enchant life when you are unaware and fearful. You can only suffer. The choice to love connects you to your original self and through it you are directly connected to the primordial energies and power of life.

## Root Tension

At the root of personal awareness (the thinking self) is a chronic tension that blocks the functional connection to the original self and so to life. The absence of life and love motivates our activities and creates our experience of life. It takes a while to realize that what we seek is not outside us, but inside us. We are eventually moved to seek an end to the tension at the root of our lives. What we discover is that nothing we do ends it—and so we continue seeking, motivated now by frustration. We have an itch we cannot ignore and cannot scratch. Tension limits attention and awareness. The thinking self is both the cause and the effect of limited awareness. Thus, the chronic mood (experiential context) of the thinking self is tension and frustration. We notice our pain and embrace it as part of our identity. We don't like living with it, but we can't imagine living without it. Thus, the dilemma of being human.

But the tension is not the problem, really. In a way it is the solution! We can end the tension by accepting it, relaxing into it, recognizing it as the natural but blocked creative energy of the original self. This allows the integration of the two selves, and so creates the functional root of enchantment. So long as we wait to experience life before we live it, before we take action, we lose the ability to enjoy life directly (before its energy is distorted by our limited awareness and generalized fear).

## Enchanted Self, Enchanted Earth

All five realms of reality are linked together. Nothing in the body or in the world is separate. As human life and the earth evolve and mature, changes echo throughout all realms. This primordial and eternal oneness has always been the case. What changes is our awareness that this is so. When you and your world are one, life becomes literally magical, enchanted. As this magic ripples through reality, the structures of our personal and collective lives shift toward deep community (beyond individuality). The current patterns of life evolve.

## The Coming Judgment

The enchantment of earth is both good news and bad news. A magical and enchanted earth is the good news, but a magical and enchanted earth is also a judgment. That is the bad news. We all dream of an idyllic future, but we also avoid it. Otherwise, it would be here already! The dream is now reality. The enchanted earth is here, emerging as we speak. Thus, our habit of avoidance and resistance will now be exposed. This is a revelation, not a condemnation. Thus, the coming judgment is really self-awareness.

An enchanted earth is emerging all around you. The price you pay for pretending this is not so is suffering, pain, even death. It is not punishment, just the result of a choice. The more literal enchantment becomes, the more you must struggle to avoid it. Eventually, the struggle can and will kill you, literally.

The problem with freedom is making choices. You must decide not only who you are, what you want, and where and how you want to live, but also whether or not you want to do all of that. Are you willing to adapt to life in a magical world? Are you able to make peace with it? Can you release childish ways in favor of a more mature, less self-obsessed life? You will judge yourself fit or not fit. You will decide, no one else.

## The Price of Enchantment

Death is the price of enchantment. It is not optional. It is unavoidable. The price for evolution has always been death of the separated selves and the whole of your life connected to it. If that is not appealing, you can try to avoid enchantment, and be overwhelmed by the coming storm of evolutionary intelligence. Either way, the result is the same. Death is in the air. Enchantment is here.

What happens when the thinking self dies? Well, that depends. The death can be externalized, literal, physical. That happens when you do not awaken from your story. But death can be internalized. It can be a death of the functional barriers between the thinking self and the original self. You transcend death by internalizing it. If you resist evolution, tension builds that demands release (change). When that change finally occurs, it can be traumatic enough to result in physical injury or death. Physical death has never been the price of evolution. It has always been the price of avoiding it. The alternative to internalizing death, to deep energetic change, is physical death. So choose: physical death, or the death of your self.

## If You Can See the Dark, You Are in the Light

Darkness appears in your life when you turn from the light of intelligence. You need not search for that light. It is already here. So, will you destroy yourself in the presence of what you desire? Ignorance (ignoring reality) cannot survive the light of intelligence. So, you can evolve or perish. Instances of self- and mutual-annihilation, global crises, are evidence people would rather die than adapt to the demands of intelligence. If you see that darkness, you are already moving toward the light of enchantment. Awareness of the insanity of global conditions is testimony of both our resistance to enchantment, and of its increasing presence in our world.

The heaven that traditions say exists beyond our grasp in this life has always been within our grasp if we will sacrifice the smallness of life for a magical and mythical life. What we have pursued individually (an empowered, magical life), now pursues us collectively. Ordinary life is sacred play, evolutionary drama.

## The End of an Age

Enchantment is the merging of the ordinary (the thinking self) and the sacred (the original self). We are witnessing the end of an age, the end of an evolutionary stage, and the birth of a new way of being human, a new kind of human being—a luminous, magical, intelligent being. The higher, more spiritual, realms are here, now, in this world, in us! We are evolving into enchanted beings in an enchanted land. There is no spiritual realm higher than earth! You need not seek enchantment in other realms of awareness because they are all here, in ordinary life. Just look.

Throughout history it has been the hope of good people that good would triumph over evil. It has never happened because our history is the drama of our separated selves generating a world where we are separated from the magic of life itself. When we focus our attention and interest on the thinking self, all we experience is a desperate search for the power and goodness, the magic, of life. Now the intelligence of life is overwhelming us. But the new age will not be without problems.

## Can You Live with Only Love?

Good people have said that justice is overcoming injustice. What a pity. That means justice is always a struggle. If the struggle for justice is the pattern of your life, you will find the arrival of enchantment disconcerting. Indeed, it is legitimate to ask if conventionally good people can survive in a truly good world. How will you live when the life-long and historical battle for goodness and justice ends? You need worry only if you root your goodness in overcoming its absence. The motivational source for your life has ended. It is just a matter of time before it is obvious to you.

How do you live an enchanted life? In love! It is simple, obvious, and not believable. There must be something more to it! What do people do in love? They relax because they are safe. They trust because they are in love. They embrace life because they are loved.

## Morality: The Conspiracy Against Love

Love is the theoretical but not the true root of morality. Morality is the effort to define what love is and how it is expressed. Good luck! Love expresses the inherent good of the original self. Morality expresses only the apparent good of the thinking self. Love is the body's natural relationship to life. It is not an activity. It is not about doing the right thing. It is about being in right relationship to life. Love is the embrace of life, not an effort to control life or yourself. Love occurs spontaneously, unavoidably, when the body is self-congruent, unconflicted. Loving behavior cannot be predicted, nor encoded in precepts or law. When love is expressed, it is creative, unselfconscious, congruent in all five realms.

Morality, on the other hand, is an effort to control behavior (physical realm) through what we believe (personal realm) usually about the gods (mythic realm). Morality is clearly rooted in a conflict within the body, and between the self and life generally. Morality happens when you try to domesticate love. Love is the life song of a wild and untamed heart. Morality is the dirge of a fearful mind.

Moralists hate the idea that love is relational, relative. It destroys the basis for morality. It disconnects love from the presumption of higher authority. This destroys the illusion that morality has roots in absolute authority derived from the mythic organizing and loving energies of the gods. It disallows our codes of moral conduct. Love is indeed relative, relational. To find it, you must look beyond the thoughts and actions of the thinking self directly into the original self. We already recognize this when we nod to a difference between the letter of the law (morality), and the spirit of the law (virtue).

## Morality Is Not Virtue

Love arises as the thinking self and the original self merge. Morality tries to make love predictable and consistent, without the need for merging. Morality is about social control. The tragic moral dilemmas in life and literature are often about this conflict between love (integrity) and morality (social law).

Morality is the dumbed-down version of love. Making love predictable destroys it. Those who espouse morality have no interest in love, only social order. And so we are disenchanted people living disenchanted lives in a disenchanted world.

Injustice is anything out of relationship to the whole (the five realms). Morality is supposed to prevent injustice, but because it only acknowledges the physical realm (behavior), it cannot recognize injustice nor respond to it in any other realm. The difference between morality and injustice is entirely arbitrary.

When we identify with the thinking self, we separate from our original self, and disconnect from life. The result is morality, which may serve the need for social order, but not love. Morality is the corruption and loss of love—the very definition and root of tragedy. A moral life is unavoidably tragic.

People do not view a moral life as tragic, but as a noble confrontation with injustice. Same thing! In such a confrontation, you supposedly rise above your daily concerns to demonstrate and validate your morality (socially and legally accepted behavior). But this is tragic for two reasons. First, morality is about behavior, not love. Morality is at best an approximation of love. So love is lost, which is tragic. Second, morality always occurs within the context of injustice. Morality is the struggle to overcome injustice. But since injustice is the necessary context for the struggle, it can never be overcome. Thus, morality becomes an endless and pointless struggle—tragedy again.

## The Defeat of Love

So, how do we live in love? The struggle to love occurs when we disconnect from our original self—the body, our biological intent to love. Suffering is then unavoidable, as is struggling. The separated and excluding nature of the unawakened thinking self is the basis for our tragic and unloving experience of life. Human experience is filled with suffering and struggling by choice, not nature. Of course, having removed enchantment from life, we want it back to end our suffering. We set the conditions for tragedy and then try to escape it. So, searching for what we have lost and can never find (because we have thrown it away) becomes a way of living. Is it not tragic? Defeat in this life is certain. A final end to our search is possible only elsewhere (we hope). Thus, tragedy becomes the mood of all human endeavor.

When human life begins with the death of love as the context of ordinary life, the only way it can end is in tragedy. Our only choice is how to dramatize a life without love. How will love be defeated?

## The Defeat of Meaning and Purpose

The struggle for love is a struggle for meaning and purpose. We sense the arbitrariness of our life and desperately seek some reason to be alive, a way to make choices that is not arbitrary and already doomed.

Once we delude ourselves that the absence of love in human affairs is not our choice but the natural condition of life, we immediately realize that our lives are unsafe. The perception that love is not the natural root of human life motivates our struggle against life in order to find love! Of course, our struggle against life separates us from love, and so we have a self-fulfilling tragedy.

If love is not the true nature of life, then morality can only be a temporary respite from that truth. The struggle for love offers the illusion of purpose in a world presumed to be without it. If we struggle for love, life becomes a noble tragedy. So, does life have meaning and purpose apart from what we impose for our own purposes? Yes! And the answer to both is the same: love.

## The Vast Left and Right Wing Conspiracy

With a purpose for life (moral struggle) that consumes all our effort for all our life, individual and social life is given order (if not purpose). Those who most dramatically enact the tragedy of love's loss and defeat become martyrs. They offer hope while confirming the futility of ordinary life. They rekindle our dream of love and help us to be content with the tragic reality of its absence.

When cultures organize around the idea that love is synonymous with struggle, life becomes an endless battle with reality for a dream that never comes true. Since there is no meaning or purpose to life beyond our selves then, the only real task in life is to survive. After all, who wants to die? Community and cooperation are just ways to ensure personal survival.

Indeed, the whole of life is now personalized. Everything is valued for its utility for personal survival and comfort. Mistrust between individuals and communities cannot be reconciled. The individual uses the community to survive, while the community uses the individual to ensure its survival. Each would gladly betray the other for its own sake.

If love is impossible, then so is happiness. We struggle for happiness just as we struggle for love, and we settle for pleasure. Work becomes drudgery, organized by boredom and fear. Frustration becomes motivation. Creativity is valued if it is marketable. Invention means novelty. Aggression is admired for generating progress. And joy is seen to undermine hard work! Peace and quiet, viewed as inaction and nonproduction, are frivolous personal indulgences. The personal qualities we admire are those that keep us struggling—but for what? Is this what we really want? Global tragedy? Are we not dramatizing our self-imposed miseries to each other?

But what happens when we make another choice, when love wins the day? We have comedy, not tragedy. The word comedy denotes triviality. So we know right away nothing important is at stake. In comedy we are happy for the moment, but we quickly forget our small joys. We cheer the good guys, hail the hero, and then go home to take out the trash. Unlike tragedy, there is no call to love in comedy. Even in comedy, life is a tragedy with comic interludes. So the hero does battle and wins the day. We admire, from a safe distance. Our focus is survival, not love. We like to think victory over suffering and injustice is possible, but we don't believe it. After all, it is just a comedy. We find the cloud in the silver lining.

## Martyrs as Heroes

The most admired and remembered times in history that call forth our greatest sympathy for love come from events we call tragic. The purpose of tragedy is to call forth qualities that were dramatically vanquished. Our natural response to tragedy is to align our lives with the qualities we saw defeated, to fill the void left by defeated love. We are moved to join the struggle that will never see victory.

Tragedy is more important than comedy. It demands analysis, deep consideration. It forcefully enters our mind to confront our own condition. Those who do not rise to the tragic occasion, the dramatization of death and ultimate impotence in life—who choose to survive—live forgotten, desperate lives. They are weaklings, untested. They lack moral fiber. They do not step up to the confrontation with injustice. Their lives are meaningless because nothing of consequence is affirmed or denied. Nothing is at stake. No sacrifice is made, no principle dramatized, nothing bequeathed. Thus, we ask some among us to protect us from the absence of love so we can survive. We honor their predictably tragic efforts with accolades, ceremonies, noble words. But their loss of life is not the real tragedy. The real tragedy is that it is all unnecessary. We intend the game of life to be tragic. Those we have sacrificed are victims of that choice.

Those who heed the call to tragedy are the redeemed and remembered. They express human nobility and save us the trouble. Their tragedy is our redemption. Their sacrifice saves us from the moral struggle. We live vicariously. We accept the bequest of their life and achieve some sense of nobility in our own life by remembering and admiring them.

We admire martyrs because even though they were defeated, their virtue and nobility remain intact through the purity of their sacrifice. The martyr redeems his otherwise meaningless life through sacrifice on the altar of love, which is attained only in death. Every martyr, then, invigorates the continuing moral struggle through his or her sacrifice. But all we really get, what we settle for, is a moral *drama*, living theater. We have heroes to dramatize our tragic purpose in life.

## A Call to Love

Are heroes and martyrs only victims, then? Can their sacrifice be redeemed? Yes! But the sacrifice of martyrs calls us to a change of heart, not behavior. But then a good question arises: Do you want love that is private and not public, where there is no test or reward? Are you interested in a life with nothing to prove, or improve, nothing to seek, no one to impress? Can you live a good life without a moral struggle?

What happens when the internal tensions that motivate you finally resolve? What will you do, how will you live, when the day is won, the party is over, and the guests have all gone home? Can you be happy then? Can you be happy in a world of peace and justice, community, freedom, love? Are these just dreams to console you during your self-imposed and unnecessary exile from life? Do you secretly want your dreams to be frustrated so you can blame reality for your life rather than accept responsibility for it?

## A Call to Inner Revolution

Enchantment is sustained only in the lives of enchanted beings. If this is what you want, then accept it now. Give up your dreams and plans. Stop focusing on the future. It has arrived. Forget your need to be right, perfect, or just new and improved. Accept your life with all its apparent imperfections and assume, as an act of love, that under the shroud of your fear that enchantment isn't true, you are indeed an enchanter in an enchanted land. The way to enchantment is not to struggle, but to suspend disbelief, to eagerly jump into the play of ordinary life as the theater of love.

Your enchanted life begins the moment you quit assuming love must be a goal! Relinquish your sense that life is a tragedy. Abandon whatever obstructs your immediate embrace of life. Only with the presumption of love can you heal yourself, others, and the planet. It is all an act of faith. Now is the time of your most harsh judgment, your most basic choice: tears or laughter? What will you do—or believe? Your choice is your destiny. Choose well.

## Ending Your Search for Love

Here's a simple but real question: How do you spend your time? What are you doing with your life? Now ask yourself why? None of us likes to think we are unaware of what we are doing and why. But a real question begs to know if you believe all you say, and if all you believe is true. Do you say and believe what is true, or just what is convenient, habitual? A real question is always simple. But if you ask yourself a real question, and demand a real answer, it will stop your life. So, people don't ask real questions nor give real answers. A real question and a real answer are the mechanism of your conversion to love.

Real questions stop your life. Real answers change your life. Real questions don't prevent you from living. They just ask you to choose before you continue. A real question is not part of your typical day. It makes your head spin, maybe hurt. You may even discover you have no real answer to a real question. Perhaps you cannot distinguish between what is real and what is merely convenient to do, feel, believe.

The problem with a real question is that you can only answer the question by self-awareness and self-recognition. A real question asks you to look beyond what you know to what you see, to go from conception to perception. And so we come to the search.

We organize our lives by searching. It is not a response to life but a way to organize it. What are we seeking? Name something! We are just hunters and gatherers, looking for what will help us survive and prosper. Reduced to the most basic patterns, life is a matter of cause and effect in pursuit of survival and prosperity. The search is about how to do that. What do we need to survive and prosper? As we search, though, we realize the question is not about physical survival and material wealth.

If we ask what motivates our search, we might say survival and prosperity, but if we look deeper, we see our real motivation is a subtle and profound sense of suffering and fear. Something about ourselves and the world is not right. We search for what will scratch our itch. We cannot let life be.

We search until we realize we are chasing our own tail. We can stop searching, but then what do we do? How do we live without searching for a way to end our suffering? As we become aware of that constant itch, we desperately want it to end. So, perhaps, we try love (or something else). Of course, it does not work, but before we dismiss it perhaps we notice our practice of love was not honest, real. It was just a trick to end our suffering, not to truly love. It was an effort to outsmart life. Love cannot end your suffering if that is your purpose. Then it is just another way to act out your drama of suffering. So we learn a good lesson: no action motivated by suffering can end it!

If you are separated from anything, you are wounded. A wounded self enacts suffering. The thinking self does not have a wound. It is the wound! Every experience occurs in the context of suffering. Your life is organized by suffering. You may experience the pain of suffering, but that is not the suffering itself. The suffering of which I speak occurs before the thinking self is aware. The only cure is to let the thinking self die (collapse into your original self). Without the relief of death, your search continues.

## Choosing Enchantment

Earth is an enchanted land. To experience that, you must make a preemptive choice. All things are present or absent by choice. Nothing else organizes your life. So, to live on any basis other than love and trust is to presume you are not experiencing your own choices. The presumption generates the reality. A presumption other than love disempowers you and delays the realization of your deepest dreams.

Reality is a mechanism to manifest your purpose. Of course, the original self makes the most powerful choice and has the most influence on your experience of life. It sets the default context for experience, which is love. To manifest your purpose without conflict, align it with the intent to love of the original self. Choose love, relentlessly.

# Living Without a Net

When our two selves merge, we experience the whole of life in all realms as us. We are infinite, a multi-verse of energies and possibilities. Yet everything we do tends to separate us from, rather than connect us to, the original self, and so life itself.

## The Practice of Love: Uncritical Awareness

Relaxed and unfocused attention is how the thinking self practices love. It generates awareness without barriers or boundaries, the context for enchantment. This uncritical acceptance frees the functions of the brain to organize in patterns consistent with the habit of the brainstem to love, to remain open and unafraid of life. Interestingly, this does not produce an experience. It alters the context and so the possibilities of experience. It enhances the quality and content of experience. The effect of uncritical awareness is indirect, yet profound. Love seeks nothing, produces nothing, but it accepts and integrates everything. Love is not an experience. It is the qualitative context of experience.

## Beyond Worship

Generally, religious worship seeks to accept the Presence of a Power from which the worshipper is presumed to be separated. In a single breath a worshipper seeks to embrace what is presumed to be absent.

Worship represents an archaic and undemocratic paradigm of power. The metaphors of worship presume inequality of power and authority. Worship suggests obedience, not love; dependence, not freedom. And this gets to the heart of the matter. Worship is a purposeful effort to affirm dependence and renounce power as part of any definition of humanness. Of course, without power, nothing happens. Thus, while worshippers renounce their power, secular and religious institutions seek and abuse it.

Worship prevents the enchantment of life by preventing the integration of the divided Self. It presumes, and so institutionalizes, the experience and perspective of the divided Self (separation from life/God). Only the undivided Self has the power to enchant life.

## Life Is Dangerous When It Is Simple

The enchantment of life ends the need for spiritual practices, insight, or experiences. Love is the means of enchantment. All that we think, feel,

35

experience, do, say, know, or practice occurs in the context of our personal purpose. When we trust our original self we trust, and so embrace or love, life in its fullness. In that context, everything we are naturally inclined to do manifests the body's intent of love. Without the purpose to love, everything we are naturally inclined to do expresses disenchantment.

Without faith (acting on your trust of the body's intent), spiritual methods, practices, and rituals are illusions. They pacify the mind and gratify the search, but they do not enchant life. All methods can do is reinforce your disenchantment. We expect to achieve our goals through perfect practice, powerful techniques, highly developed skills. But enchantment is the outcome of relentless love. Period.

All forms of spiritual or religious practice complicate life and delay its enchantment. Ordinary life (in the context of the relentless purpose to love) is spiritual practice! There is not something you do to make life spiritual. Life already is spiritual, in love. Love is the best and only true spiritual practice.

Life is radically simplified when your only strategy for living is love. Such simplicity makes you both powerful and dangerous. In love, you don't need a net to save you from the dangers of life. You are an enchanter in an enchanted land. That is the message.

## Conversion: The Power of Intent

To transform your life and the world, convert your life to love as your purpose. Then act as if it were true. How can this change the root of your life? Well, the brainstem does not separate your inner life from reality. There is a constant two-way flow of energetic information between the body and reality, through the brainstem. And the thinking self has no experience of reality except through the original self. The body enacts an implicit intention to love all of life. What you dream inwardly becomes true outwardly.

Enchantment occurs when your natural but unconscious inclination to embrace reality becomes consciously enacted without inhibition, when you let down your guard and get out of your head. That happens when you relax! Simple.

Notice and release any distrust or fear. Choose to interpret your experiences as evidence of love, even and especially when this seems not to be true. Why do this? Aren't you just deluding yourself? Of course! But your dream of love is already a biological fact. Relax, accept, and presume a magical life in a magical land. It is literally true. By not fearing life, you experience the truth that life is love. Trust your body. Get with the program! All experience is an illusion. What illusion would you prefer?

## Faith Is Relentless

Faith is another word for relaxing, trusting life without doubt, concern, or fear. Thus, faith empowers love. Faith gives the body conscious permission to love. As you can imagine, faith is not easy. Simple, but not easy. You must practice allowing the natural inclination of the body to love to overwhelm and overcome the unloving habits you have forced upon it through your practice of fear and distrust. Let the body heal itself and the mind. You will experience your wounds as fear, doubt, rage, tears, an inability to trust. Love is the healing balm for a disenchanted life. Faith lets the healing begin.

The relentless love of the body overcomes all barriers to life. All things change, but the habit of love embedded in your nervous system is the one constant in your life. Relax. Let love overwhelm you!

## Faith Opens the Door, Love Walks In

Love is a biological habit of the nervous system. The presumption of love is a mental act of surrendering to a pre-existing biological fact. This allows the nervous system to function without resistance from the thinking self. The first result, mentioned earlier, is conversion—the inward and upward movement of energy into the nervous system that begins the evolutionary journey of love. Next, the habits of the upper brain begin to heal, accommodating energetic increases as the brain is also functionally re-wired. The result is the enlightenment of the mind. This is followed in turn by enlightenment of the heart (the mid-brain), and enlightenment of the body (brainstem), the outward and downward flow, or outpouring, of energy from the body to the world, which creates magic. Make love your only purpose. Then trust the sacred healing play that results. The thinking self must practice this relentlessly until tensions relax and love overwhelms you.

Prior to enlightenment, your life intent to love (held in the brainstem) is unknown to the thinking self. You are unaware of it. You only know what you hope is true. So your practice of faith must evolve from a mere conscious desire to love into bodily relaxation, which alone allows the original self to manifest love in the mind, body, and world, in that order. Faith alone cannot connect the two selves without relentless practice. Why? Because subconscious emotional habits stand in the way and must be overcome through a relentless and conscious practice of relaxation and trust.

As you practice faith, fears and inhibitions come to awareness, and so become available for healing. The depth of your fears may surprise you. It is only such healing that can transform your capacity to love. So, attend to what you really want, because what you want controls what you will trust.

## There Can Be Only One

Human beings have only one intention in life: love. Human history is testimony to what happens when we fight that natural inclination and our only true purpose in life. Enchantment depends on the singularity of your intent to love. It demands that you have no other purpose to fulfill in life, no other reason for being. Enchantment occurs when the whole of your life is organized around love, only love. Trying to live any other purpose only sets up a conflict with the original self. You become unintelligent, unloving. You struggle. Enchantment is served and fulfilled by having only one purpose.

As you practice faith, you will discover your life has a life of its own, first expressing a variety of neurotic needs and habits, but gradually giving way to a natural intelligence. This is the original self, your true passion and life intent, healing any limit on love.

## Living Your Dream

What if your purpose is not enchantment? Then find and embrace your true purpose, passion, dream. This will always be some expression of love. Surrender to love. You will be miserable until you do. When you do, embrace life and let the power of life fulfill your dream in the context of love. Love is the most powerful context in which to live your dream and the only context in which living your dream is truly fulfilling. Seek your heart's desire in sincerity and innocence. Then be open to the possibilities of life.

Do not worry about living your dream. End the habit of imposing a goal on your life. What we achieve is less important than how we live. Life is a play, not a race. Our goals express mostly our fear about what life will fail to provide. Love is the source of all worthy dreams and the power to live them. So, let faith connect you to your body's original and only intent and let your dreams emerge from there. As you surrender to the passion of love, you will find anything is possible and all good things inevitable.

# Conversion: Crossing the Threshold of Love

Each moment we presume love, we undermine the conflict between our separated selves. This alters the habits of your nervous system. It shifts the location of your identity from thinking self to original self. Conversion is not a declaration of religious affiliation. It is a choice to alter how you interpret experience, which ultimately changes how the body-mind processes the information you interpret.

Religious conversion alters the ecology of the thinking self only. It organizes the contents of the thinking self through beliefs, reinforcing an exclusive identification with the thinking self and continued separation from the original self. Your behavior may change through self-conscious effort to comply with these self-imposed beliefs, but the two selves remain separated, conflicted. Brain functions remain neurotic, disorganized. And so you remain separated from the world around, from love. True conversion occurs in the body, not the mind. It alters the ecology of your entire inner life.

Enchantment = the body's intent of love + the mind's purpose to love + deep faithful action consistent with love. Love is in each experience, ready to inform us, guide us, delight us. All we seek can be found in everything we have. Your body trusts life. The problem is that you don't. Experience reflects what you are willing to experience, your purpose. The mood and pattern of your life will change when you alter what you believe is possible and relax.

## The Psychology of Faith

The subconscious mind is anything you hold below the awareness threshold of the thinking self. Its contents are held throughout the body, not just in the brain. Anything suppressed or unloved limits awareness, and so your capacity to give and receive love.

As we relax, the subconscious mind empties. The learned inhibitions of our nervous system are undermined. Faith grows. Generally, we trust life where we have no wounds, no issues to resolve, or inhibitions to overcome. When we relax, we feel uneasy because we enter into areas where we have unacknowledged fears and wounds. To remain in such discomfort is not yet justified by experience. So, we pull back into our comfort zone. We fail to love because we do not trust our inner life. We have disowned our original self. The only solution is to persist in the purpose of love despite your concerns.

How can you prepare for a life of love? You can't! It is a matter of purpose. You are ready when you decide to be. That you are here, alive, on earth, means you are ready, but you must be ready by choice.

## Your Conversion to Love

Your spiritual path is whatever you avoid or do not love. Your true spiritual path is not a formulaic practice of love. It is your willingness to embrace and heal all that you now avoid. This practice encourages either love or cynicism. It is your choice.

Your lessons on the path of love are stark reminders that your choice not to love has immediate consequences—no small voice pleading with you to try again. Love is more muscular than that! Life is a play of tough love. It is about action (inward and outward, above and below) and its results, nothing else. Life is the interaction between your choices and those of others. Life presumes you know what you are doing. (Talk about faith!). Life trusts you with the power to live your choices, even when you do not know you have power or choices. The price you pay for not knowing what you want, or what you are doing, is suffering. How else could it be? How else should it be? Life does not kibitz, suggesting ever so nicely that you might like things a bit more by doing this instead of that. Life does not care if your life, or the theater of life itself, offends you. Life allows you, and expects you, to deal with it!

Reaping what you sow, loving what you have not loved before, continues until there is a stable congruence between your two selves and your outer life, until you learn to be inwardly what you want to experience outwardly. This continues until your conversion from fear to love is complete, absolute, without conditions: enchantment.

Are you ready for the enchantment of life on earth? Yes, if you intend to embrace life despite your lack of readiness. Even if you are not prepared to confront some past issue or encounter some new truth, if you are willing, you are prepared. If readiness has nothing to do with being prepared, then readiness is about courage more than skill. Yes! It is about learning, not avoiding mistakes. There is no preparation for life. Your birth, an act of courage and faith itself, is your readiness.

## Spiritual Teachers

Spiritual teachers are unnecessary for enchantment, enlightenment, or evolution, despite what traditions or teachers say. They are unnecessary, but they can be valuable. That said, the teacher-student relationship is often a mutual addiction, both parties acting from their needs and wounds. Spiritual teachers are often unconfessed, incomplete beings.

Spiritual teachers can serve you in two ways. They can serve you before and after your conversion to love. The difference is responsibility. Before conversion, your reason to pursue a spiritual path and a teacher can be anything. So, a teacher should help you toward conversion (to love in life, not a tradition). But that is not often what happens.

In conversion, you take responsibility for your evolution. You end dependence on a spiritual teacher or tradition. Conversion is an energetic rite of passage that moves you from adolescent dependence on a spiritual parent to mature independence and responsible equality among friends.

After conversion, the role of teacher changes to companion, mature spiritual friend. Your relationship is whatever you decide or create. You assume responsibility for a direct and independent connection to life, in communion with others. The companion's job is to support your conversion, so your power and insight make a valuable and stable contribution to the relationship. Conversion makes a huge difference in the nature of the relationship that is possible with a spiritual friend. Before conversion, other practitioners cannot take you into their communion because you have no purposeful relationship to your original self. Conversion changes that. Of course your conversion will be tested to ensure it is stable. Conversion aligns you with life, not the teacher. After conversion, the teacher is an accessory to evolution, not its source.

## Making the Choice to Convert

Conversion is choosing to alter the habits of your nervous system, to transform how the information of life gets to you, what information gets to you, and how it is interpreted. You preempt your fears and history and identity with love. But choices are often unstable. You may doubt the value of practicing love because it is difficult. You waffle. Your good intentions collapse in the face of your fears. But then you make yourself accountable for your choice. You no longer question your choice, only your sincerity.

Conversion is a choice prompted by an awakening. You see life is inescapable. You accept it. You quit the struggle. You capitulate to the obvious. The mind relaxes and falls into the heart.

## Ending the Search

Searching prevents love. The search begins and continues when you believe there is something in life not yet available to you. So long as you think there is something to be achieved, some defect to improve, something yet to know, you will never convert to love. Your practice will be hesitant, troubled, in doubt, and your experience of life will reflect all of that. The only lesson to learn before conversion is that all you seek is already here. Decide when to believe this and you will know your future. Love is the only life strategy that is inherently free and freeing. Any other choice conflicts with your own body.

## Conversion Through Spiritual Experiences

You might think you should wait for a spiritual experience before converting your life to love. This is true of religious conversions. But you are as ready to convert before an experience as you are afterwards. How so? Conversion requires a choice, even after an experience! It might be easier to put off choosing, but what are you really waiting for?

## Converting from Little Me to Big Me

Conversion to love is the last act of a disenchanted life. It is the first act of your life in love. You might approach love as part of a process of self-improvement, but this will not lead to enchantment. Love results in personal and even global transformation beyond the patterns and concerns typical of ordinary life. It is not a way to enhance ordinary life. It is a way to transform it utterly, to the cellular level, literally. Do not practice love as part of some other effort. If you will not surrender into the energetic roar and play of life, you are not ready for a life of enchantment.

You might expect to control and direct the course of your evolutionary learning. Let go of that idea! Love is the way to become what you already are, not whatever you think you want or ought to be. The kinds of choices you seek to make are a part of an enchanter's life, but only after you have been thoroughly transformed in the fires of love. Only when you are fully a part of life in all realms can you be trusted with those kinds of choices.

Evolution requires an intricate and deep level of healing that can be initiated by the thinking self (in conversion) but not directed by it. You must surrender the thinking self in every moment to love (the habit of the original self). Love is our original and only true spiritual path. That path leads to the enchantment of all life on earth. Its demands are uncompromising and nonnegotiable.

In the first age of humankind
The age of the body and childhood,
We lived to survive.

# The Life of Enchantment

## How Evolutionary Learning Works

FIRST LET US CONSIDER WHAT YOU are doing before we proceed. Perhaps you see images or hear stories of bliss, an end to suffering. But images and stories do not sustain you in the evolutionary fires of love. Evolution ruins your life! You cannot justify a pursuit of personal and global transformation. It makes no sense. It is a calling, a deeply felt imperative, obvious to some, invisible to most. You either hear the call or you don't. If you do, you cannot and dare not ignore it. Do you hear the disquieting call of life?

Love is its own imperative. Love is not something you choose. It chooses you! If you need to justify it, stop! The choice to love until evolution cannot be justified by conventional wisdom.

### The Moment Before You Exist

To love to the point of enchantment, you must love directly. That means in every moment there are really four moments: the moment of intention, faith (mythic level), attention (personal level), and the moment of action (physical level). To live directly, you must live in the moment of intention or origination, the first moment. Before faith, perception, thought, or action, there is the moment of the body's intent. There is the fire of the Primordial Spirit. There is the moment of enchantment.

By not living in the first moment, you are living your life after the important choices have been made. You are not living your own life. Someone or something else is creating your world. Is this what you want?

Those who live in the moment of intention create the world the rest of us inhabit. Such people create the energetic paradigm, the mythic archetypes, that organize and create our world and set the scope of possibilities for the rest of us. That paradigm is now the possibility of enchantment. Did you notice?

Those who forego improving their personal life to surrender fully into life without boundaries or barriers are human beings, not super beings, just human beings. They disregard the limits and conventions of life. They find no way to constrain life. They are seized by the untamed heart of life. They swoon in its embrace. They become what they love. They do not love the truth. There is no truth. There is only life. But they do love truly, fully. They do not advocate a way of life. They advocate life itself, before we try to improve it, when it is still a grace and joy, and not a duty.

The simplicity, the power, the joy and love of life is available in our world, in our time, when you live directly. It is not an evolutionary step back. It is a step back into life. It is we, in this world and time, that have stepped back from life and become lost in the marvels of the mind. Now it is time to step back into the roaring current of life. It is possible to live in the moment before life becomes complicated, without going back to the Stone Age. That life is the stuff of dreams. The price of getting there is your life.

## Energetic and Biological Learning

Intelligence is learned! Evolutionary intelligence is biological. It is for the courageous warrior, not the precise intellectual. Evolutionary learning is a deeply moving, personal journey into the unknown, within and without. It is important to acknowledge that enchantment cannot be discussed! Words always fail. Life and enchantment are bigger than our ideas. So all our ideas about enchantment are basically untrue. To understand enchantment, we must encounter it without our ideas.

We do not really see life. We see what we know, believe, have been told, remember. We do not see ourselves. We cannot be ourselves. What can be done? How can we escape our trance to make a choice if only to go back? The skill most conducive to awakening is love. Until we love before we know, we can neither see nor learn anything new. So how does life encourage us to move beyond our limits? Pain and suffering. Works for me! When we need to change but do not have the courage for it, we experience life's repeated insistence (suffering) until we relent. It is amazing how good we feel when it is over!

Love embraces the impossible, the irrational. To love, then, suspend your disbelief of things not known, perceived, or experienced. Suspension of disbelief (love) opens the door to a wider life. Evolution occurs automatically, given a release from doubts and fears. But suspension of disbelief releases tension as the boundaries of what is possible in your life are deliberately expanded. This tension is the experience of death when it is internalized. The tension results from the lack of love and resolves immediately as you surrender your fear of change. You experience tension and pain when change occurs without love.

Love is the antidote to all things born of the mind. Love clears the mind of content, leaving it open, accepting what is present, able to learn from your life without reference to history or belief, able to directly perceive life in the first moment. Love allows for the purely energetic learning that can only occur before the moments of perception, conception, and action. It is biological learning. This is the quickest and most profound form of learning. It promotes evolution, not knowledge. When learning is energetic, the mind is aware of change only after it happens. So, it cannot protect you! O-o-o-o-oh.

## How to Learn Energetically

There is in many cultures a bias against education and learning. It stems from the premise that learning implies imperfection, inadequacy, personal weakness. If you need to learn, you are already stupid. Learning is what you do when you have been wrong. Competence ends the need to learn. Those who find it most difficult to learn energetically think they already know. For others, there is a conscious choice against awareness, especially about personal issues. Either way, there is a commitment against learning. Such people do not live life. They survive it.

Learning is not about knowledge. Teaching is not about presenting it. If they were, learning would be memorization and teaching would be indoctrination. Sound familiar? Teaching can be structured, learning cannot. Learning is a free, immediate, spontaneous, and sincere response to life, possible only in a context of love. To learn energetically, you must be fully present and open in the moment. Learning without love makes you intellectually and personally defensive. You quest for something, anything, that fits with what you already know and think. In this way, you become an apologist for your own story.

Since life is multi-dimensional, so must learning be. Thus, what you learn may have no obvious connection to what is taught. As a learner, you must be willing to go where the moment leads. You may think you are tracking a thought or a feeling, but what you are really tracking is the scent of evolution.

When you attend learning events, your hopes and fears also attend. You arrive full of yourself. Your mind is full—unable, even if willing, to cross the threshold of love to befriend the unknown. Given this personal fortress against learning, teaching must break down these formidable barriers. If you are committed to being your story, then learning demands that the perfection of you and your story be confirmed. So, you are not there to learn, to change. Learning is code for consolation and congratulation. Think motivational talk!

In the unfortunate event the teacher presumes you are there to learn, a confrontation arises. You object to anything new, to what you do not already know, understand, or believe. You question the teacher, not as a way of learning, but as a way to object, to argue your point, to defend your story and sense of reality.

Learning occurs when barriers to learning collapse. You must be vulnerable, naïve, childlike. But that is the last thing you want. Such unselfconsciousness is embarrassing, revealing. Besides, you lose focus and control. (Not good!). Real learning does not satisfy the formidable need to be perceived as the pinnacle of evolution! Please note, this encounter between teacher and learner is not peculiar to that relationship. The struggle between evolutionary learning and the need for personal justification is the pattern of our life!

How can this be avoided? Evolutionary learning requires a direct and independent relationship with life, not mediated by the mind, least of all another person. Learning means forgetting your story and embracing life: a conversion from fear to love. You must directly perceive this moment to learn energetically. But perception is not about knowing. Learning is not about knowing. It is about love.

If other people assist your evolution, the conversion to love is critical. Otherwise learning depends on them, or their words and ideas. You cannot test their knowledge or story against your life. You can only test their story against your own. Learning becomes a struggle over stories. Enchantment is lost.

Love must be more than trusting a teacher, or book, or even your mind. You must trust life. To keep learning from being mere consolation, you must develop a direct relationship with life. This is how you learn energetically. It is how you keep formal or conceptual education from becoming indoctrination.

## The Illusion of Learning from Human Teachers and Saviors

All of this applies especially to spiritual and religious teachers or gurus! Learning must be independent of teaching. The learner must be free of the teacher from the start. Thus, embrace learning as your core process in life. Be available to learning at all times. The key to evolutionary learning is not getting the right teacher or teaching. In love, your relationship to life is a learning relationship. Everything and everyone is your teacher. But this does not preclude collaborative learning with a particular person or group.

It is not a teacher's credentials that determine the value of what they teach. It is the quality of your love. In love, you will always learn more than you are taught because your love is without limit. You are learning from life, not the teacher. It is possible you will disagree with all you are taught, dislike the teacher, yet find yourself deeply affected. Good or not, you made yourself available to the energy of the moment and it had its way with you. The teacher was merely an instrument of your learning. That is what you want! If you respond positively to the teacher, great. If not, then you have found a need for healing.

So, responsibility for learning is yours, not the teacher's! You disempower yourself if you approach teachers any other way. Do not quibble over the truth or falsity of a teacher. It does not matter. It has power and importance only for those who do not take responsibility for their learning or their lives.

In Eastern traditions, for instance, there are teachers who claim they are the Truth. They are the freedom beyond knowledge. They embody the liberating power of the Primordial Spirit. Yes, and their point is? All things are infinite. Every thing that exists is always teaching every thing that can be learned. Everything is the truth! Their statement may be a clear appeal to authority and an implicit invitation to leave your power and intuitive intelligence at the ashram door, but it does not matter. A teacher may leave you confused and abused. It does not matter. Take responsibility for your learning and choices. Such teachers are simply claiming that by dint of great effort (presumably) or by virtue of physical birth, they now enjoy the same ontological status as a rock—and that means no disrespect to the rock!

There are lots of people who can help you with evolutionary learning. Indeed, anything and everything can help. But whether someone helps you or not depends on you, not them. It is your love, or its limitations, that directs the course of your learning. It has nothing to do with them.

All of this is difficult to see when learning occurs within a guru-disciple relationship. You have no way to verify the process can occur any other way. So long as the teacher and student attribute learning to the teacher, the student is doomed to a permanent (in some traditions, eternal) subservient relationship to the teacher. It is a relationship that not accidentally disconnects you from life's great play as a source of change and learning. The enchantment of life on earth remains an eternally distant hope.

## Learning and Grace

How would you teach a child to distinguish a horse from a dog? Would you share pictures of different animals? Would you visit a ranch? Whatever you do, at some point the child must perceive the difference between horses and dogs. It is not about logic, or a simple definition would suffice. It is about perception. How to perceive a horse can be learned, but not taught. A teacher can help, but learning is a moment of perception not conception. Without direct perception, the learner must depend on the teacher.

Imagine you are in a traffic intersection and cannot distinguish a car from a house by sight. Words and definitions would be useless, even dangerous. Talk about insecurity! And then you are hit by a moving house! You learn to distrust your senses and seek a better definition of house. What's wrong with this picture? If this conceptual process was your only way to relate to the world, you would never know how much easier it is to look directly and see for yourself rather than consult definitions. Would you trust directness and simplicity if you had learned to trust only ideas? If you cannot perceive life directly, you are trapped in concepts and logic that have no necessary relationship to reality. The moment of direct seeing is a moment of enlightenment. It can be learned, but not taught.

## Direct Perception

Evolutionary learning requires direct perception, not ordinary perception. What is the difference? Imagine standing on a cliff preparing to jump into the beautiful lake below. A friend with you, however, shakes her head and says there is no lake. But it is a good day. You feel great. Life will support you. You jump without looking, trusting your direct (intuitive) perception that everything is O.K. If you instead heed your friend's claim, and look, that would be trusting ordinary perception. If you jump into each moment in fearless trust, you are living directly, in deep faith. But evolution occurs after you jump, when you realize your friend was right and you must now learn to fly!

To live directly is to live in the first moment of love, before perception or conception (they catch up later). It connects the moment of action to the moment of origination directly, skipping the moments of perception and conception. Now love directly organizes and supports your evolutionary journey.

Faith is not a guarantee against mistakes. Evolution is about learning, not perfection. Jumping off a cliff only to discover there is no lake below could be considered a mistake—if you want to go swimming! But if you seek evolution, that mistake now offers you the freedom (and the need) to evolve wings. Until that moment you did not need them. Such an evolutionary moment (crisis) occurs when you do something truly stupid. But it is only in the first moment of love (prior to all other moments), that evolution occurs. The moment of love is a moment of high risk (evolution requires courage more than faith). It is a moment of potential death (transformation). It is a moment of emptiness, so love is drawn to the moment, fills in the space, and produces a miracle—you fly!

## The Real Process of Evolutionary Learning

If evolutionary learning is so natural, what are we to make of the complex methods of the traditions? All methods of spiritual teaching and learning complicate and distract us from the more basic and inclusive process of love. Of course, love is easily subverted as a learning strategy. That is why it depends on sincerity and commitment, purpose and perseverance. The insincere person subverts all learning and teaching. Love must be your real purpose, or it fails as a learning strategy.

Love works when there is no duplicity. Love, as a learning strategy, needs you to detect insincerity, to be honest about the sincerity of your purpose. Because love is a direct, nontechnical, nonspecific way to learn, you cannot verify what you learn or even notice learning since it occurs prior to the moment of awareness. In the absence of sincerity and dedication, love only confirms your insincerity, your doubts.

Spiritual methods always express no-love. It is important to note that methods work only where there is love. But methods obstruct and limit direct learning. They change nothing. They create experiences, which slow down the learning process. So why not skip experience and go directly to learning? If your love is sincere, you will learn from more than you experience. When that happens, spiritual practices are seen for what they really are: irrelevant at best, obstructive at worst.

## The Path of Nonavoidance

Life on earth is already enchanted. We want to believe it, but we don't. Thus, we seek what is here already using methods that imply it is not. A spiritual path should end our separation from life. But there is nothing to end. We are not separated. It is only what we see. When we choose love, we see love.

A spiritual path is a way to practice what we do not really want to practice. Rather than struggle against our choices, would it not be simpler, more direct, to just stop avoiding life? Just a thought. A formal path is unnecessary and ultimately misleading. It is how we confirm our experience of alienation.

To be on a path to make life spiritual is to presume life is not spiritual, that life is not enchanted! That is a lot to presume. If you are on such a path, question and abandon that presumption because it is organizing your experience of life. Pointing to experience to confirm your presumption only proves the power of your presumption. It does not mean you are right, only that you are powerful.

Every life is a spiritual and energetic process or path. Spiritual paths then are—redundant? No, worse. A spiritual path is a way to avoid the natural and inherent spiritual path of ordinary life—love.

The blueprint for enchantment is with you in every moment, on every spiritual path. It is your body's intent to love. It is not a goal. It cannot be a goal. It is in your body, secretly influencing your life. "Wake up! Wake up!" Can you hear it? Embrace everything. Avoid nothing. That is the practice of love.

# The Heart of Life

At the moment of enlightenment, the thinking self falls into (merges with) the original self. The world of ordinary experience loses its boundaries. All experience collapses into a vast singularity that is prior to the thinking self. In that moment, there is no subject or object, nothing to experience, no one to experience it. Only when you return to the world of ordinary experience do you notice what happened. You realize that you, the thinking self, just died—ceased its separateness. You dissolved in the energetic realm. You ceased to exist as an individual and merged with the Infinite.

You might think you could induce this self-unification by focusing attention on the original self. The traditions do. But the thinking self can only observe. It cannot merge unless it stops observing (dies).

We all have lots of things we want to do, achieve, etc. But love is a unique purpose because it is inherently without boundaries, radically inclusive. So it serves well as a unifying strategy for living. But love is also unique because it is the only and inherent activity of the original self. Only love has the power to unify and enlighten our inner life while it enchants our outer life. When love is the organizing purpose of our life, all other concerns are secondary and subject to its influence.

If love is the organizing purpose of our inner life in the moment of conversion, it becomes a stable influence in our inner life with enlightenment. Love is then the organizing purpose of our personal outer life in realization. Finally, love is the context for our public life, the organizing purpose and intent of our relationships, and a stable healing influence on our bodies in the moment of enchantment.

## The Power of Presumption

We often make two assumptions about personal awareness, both of them wrong. One, we do not exist before personal awareness. Two, nothing else does either. Assumptions limit the body's intent to love.

A presumption reflects your sense of reality, identity, purpose. A presumption is your effective purpose. Here we make another mistake: we assume that our stated purpose has more influence in our life than our unexamined presumptions. *Tilt!* So, we often discover that our stated purpose conflicts with something we cannot identify that prevents us from living it. That is a conflict between our conscious desires and our secret presumptions. And all of that may conflict with the body's basic intent to love.

Another presumption is that there is nothing to know, or that can be known, beyond personal awareness. After all, if nothing exists out there, what can be known? But we live in a bigger universe than we can see or even imagine with our conventional, personal, private, pinhole view of life.

Of course, that is a presumption, an act of faith. And that is precisely the point. What sort of world do you want to live in? What sort of life do you want? It is your choice. What you presume becomes your purpose and limits what is possible, unless you presume love, which opens you to life without any limits. The world we really live in is much more interesting and benign than the world we usually presume.

The distance between an ordinary life and an enchanted life is filled with tension and fear. Those who brave the unknown that separates us from a land of enchantment have the warrior-like love of the explorer, the adventurer, the one whose dream cannot be contained in the small world of the known, whose courage compels discovery and creation. If we do not confront and embrace life with such deep courage and love, we will forever huddle around the campfire of our knowledge and stare into the darkness of an eternal night in fear. It is a shameful, unnecessary choice, and unworthy of us.

## Overwhelming Your Fears

The original self has always known what the thinking self can barely imagine. To presume this is the only doorway to enchantment. To presume this opens the door between the thinking self and the original self in both directions. This means that all your wounds, fears, and demons will be coming out to play in the theater of personal awareness. What was hidden now becomes visible.

This can be very threatening. It gets worse: The original self is wild, untamed, open to life without inhibition. Its influence is disruptive. The thinking self will no longer be in charge. But, if you make the journey to enchantment, you must allow the power and chaos of love to have its way with you.

We are intimidated, and so limited, by the unknown. It is something out there to be avoided. But when the unknown is included in our presumption of love, we have the opportunity for enchantment. We are no longer limited by its ignorance. The unknown and the Infinite have just been internalized.

To avoid the unknown in ourselves or life defeats our dreams and actually generates suffering and struggling. It does not protect us. We cannot protect ourselves from life. Avoidance of the unknown denies the possibility of the enchantment that is all about us. All of this for the sake of the illusion of security and predictability. It is not the act of a warrior, an adventurer, a lover of life. Love is living in front of each moment, in the heart. Love is living in the midst of what you do not know and do not fear.

## Commitment

In love there are shoppers and buyers, tourists and residents, aspirants and vagrants. The difference is commitment. The difference between evolution and stagnation is commitment. It is how you overwhelm resistance to love. It is the root of power, strength of character, depth of wisdom, and breadth of freedom.

Your commitment to love defines the scope of your purpose, which must be greater than the scope of your suffering. The more you suffer, the more commitment it takes to heal and end it. Your commitment is to love the fullness of life, of course, and that includes your suffering. And there is the rub. You must commit to embracing your suffering in order to heal it. You cannot heal what you do not love.

Since awareness occurs in the context of suffering, your commitment to love must precede awareness and so your experience of life. You must commit to embracing the whole of life in love. When evolution feels chaotic, its pressures too great to bear, commitment will steady your journey and save your future.

Without commitment, you will falter. Fear and doubt will convince you to turn from love, to seek consolation. Commitment carries you through trials and darkness that at times seem endless. Commitment is all that keeps you going, facing into the wind of life in this moment, until at last the chaos resolves in a climax of peace and profound joy. Commitment is courage, perseverance, determination, and faith.

Commitment helps you recognize your fears and live your dream. You commit most easily to your presumptions (fears) that prevent you from living your dreams. Thus, you can maintain no purpose or direction in life. A dream is just a wish without commitment. Commitment makes anything possible. It is how love gets traction in life. We commit to something in each moment. In each moment our purpose is whatever we seek in that moment.

Commitment is not dedication to achievement, but to purpose. It does not prevent doubts or failure. It is the will to notice all of this and return to love anyway.

Commitment is not about self-control, self-coercion, or imposing your will on anything. Without commitment, purpose has no power to organize awareness. Commitment is a constant remembering of purpose (an act of unifying). It is dedication to purpose before thought or consideration.

At times, experience overwhelms your capacity to love. When at last you return to love, that return will appear as forgiveness, not frustration or anger. Your return to love occurs as a relaxation, yet again, into the quiet embrace of the moment, knowing that the moment now serves the enchantment of life.

If commitment seems to demand self-coercion, you have not committed. You need self-coercion when you wait for your habits to appear and then assert your purpose. Do not wait. Move ahead of your fears in courage and love. Overwhelm your fears. Do not react to them. Convert your life purpose to love.

Commitment is not to keep yourself on task. It is to keep yourself on purpose. Commitment is not an excuse to scold yourself or others when you or they falter. If it is, then there is no love, only the cold comfort of personal and collective pride in effort. Love keeps commitment from becoming a burden.

Commitment to love is a moment-to-moment continuation of your conversion. It is not a vow taken once and forgotten. It is the ongoing interaction between your purpose to love and the rest. The spiritual path of ordinary life is a continuing conversion of your purpose from fear to love. Commitment to continual conversion will end your struggle with doubt and fear. Your commitment is clear. You no longer question its legitimacy. You only question its sincerity. It is not what you do. It is what you are.

Your desire for enchantment speaks to your deepest, most secret and profound yearning—the desire for a life where the problems and concerns of the ordinary are at last resolved in the sublime, glorified, and evolved possibility of enchantment. This is more than merely a personal desire. It is recognition of destiny, a collective evolutionary imperative. It is your heart calling you home to the community of the whole.

# Ecstatic Abandon

To be fully human should not require special training or effort. It should be easy, natural, unlabored, without thought or consideration, spontaneous. If your life requires self-conscious effort, then you are not truly, honestly, being human. You are trying to fulfill some inhuman image of being human. Enchantment is not about perfect beings full of eternal bliss and infinite compassion. Enchantment is ordinary people who presume love as a birthright, the natural condition of life. But love is incomplete until you embrace life with complete abandon and freedom. When you abandon yourself to life, you release life itself from the bondage of your demands, expectations, and fears. In a single moment, you free the world. You free it for healing, evolution, creativity, and prosperity. And life responds with joyful abundance.

## Overwhelming History

And now a word from our sponsor. When you embrace life rather than fear it, you release suppressed tendencies, long-forgotten memories, habits you thought and hoped were gone. Now healing can begin: your energetic history rises to awareness. Here is the touchstone for tourists in the game of life. If your conversion to love does not slam you into the wall of your personal limits, making you fully aware of them and forcing choices about how to proceed, then your purpose is not to evolve. Here is where we separate the tourists from the players in the enchanter's game. This is why so many people fear to abandon themselves to love. They fear what they harbor within. They want to be rid of it, but do not want to face it. Their practice is supposed to help them, with the added benefit that they never need to be aware of it, never have to choose anything but continuing their practice. Because of this, we have enlightened people who are totally neurotic.

The surfacing of the subconscious is another layer of personal reality being revealed. The personal and social cost of this can be high. After all, who wants to be around while you are in the midst of a messy transformation? Who wants to be around while your pent-up frustration is released into the social commons? Who wants to, or can, help you process all of this and so help you stabilize your life? Evolution does not demand therapy. Far from it. Therapy inhibits the process. Evolution does not require we sit in a circle listening to each other's tales of woe. It only requires accepting the evolutionary drama of others while we learn to internalize our own.

This is why social contracts and law arose. They protect us from our collective subconscious, from the chaos we would unleash if we gave vent without qualification to our fears. This is why spiritual literature begins with an insistence on behavioral morality. Until we have enough impulse control to abide within the framework of common decency, we are unfit for further energetic learning. Our lives must reflect a natural, unlabored decency if we are to proceed. Ecstatic abandon is not behavioral license.

# Freedom

Freedom is the absence of internal limits, not the least of which is personal delusion. You are not free when your life is compromised by unawareness. People are not free and do not know it. As evolutionary learning and healing occurs, there may be many energetic shifts in the nervous system, but you are not and cannot be truly free until the separation of the two selves has been overcome.

How can this be done? Love. How is that? Love is not entitlement or ownership! Love is not attachment. It is not consistent with exclusivity, given or received. Love is a constant giving of life energy. It is inherently free-ing and healing. Love is the wisdom and power of your original self. Since love is the body's habit, the only context in which you are not in conflict with your own body is in love. Only in love are all internal limits overcome. Only in love are external barriers overwhelmed. Only in love are the barriers between the individual and the group resolved, freeing both the individual and the group. The absence of freedom begins in the absence of love.

## Power

It is the same with power. You have vast creative power, but you are unaware of it. Love encourages self-awareness, empowering self-expression. Socially, love encourages self-expression. Thus, internal and external barriers are overcome in love.

Try not to manage or control your life right now. Do not try to direct your evolution. You do not yet have the wisdom to know what limits and what frees. Most of us would rather power out of tough situations than allow evolutionary learning and healing to occur by accepting them in love. An unloving resort to power always creates karma (unintended consequences). What best serves the interests of love does not usually serve the interests of the separated self.

## Awareness

There is never a moment when you can take your freedom for granted, without consequence. The conditions of life disallow it. We are reminded of our actions and their consequences in every moment. They linger in the air. We cannot forget responsibilities once aware of them, for we see the consequences all too clearly. We must affirm our power and freedom creatively and intelligently. We must be ever aware.

To live in freedom is to live with death, full awareness that in every moment your choices mean life or death for some aspect, some part, of the Infinite You. As an enchanter of life you straddle the threshold of life and death. This is what it means to be creative. This is what it means to choose. Death is the emptiness from which all things come and to which all things return.

However, do not concern yourself about losing what freedom and awareness you have gained. That will not happen. What does happen is that the evolutionary imperative constantly reminds you of your unawareness through unexpected consequences. Freedom has its roots in awareness. Without awareness you have no choices, and so no freedom.

## Identity

To be free means you no longer live as a channel for insight or power. You are not a channel for someone or something else, nor a solitary force separated from the rest of life. You are not speaking or living on behalf of someone or something other than your self. You are the very source of insight and power. To be free is to be fully one with the whole of life and full of your original self. You are the power of life incarnate. Your expression of life is a matter of love in the midst of ordinary life. But love is not a personal matter. You are one voice among many in the choir of life.

Freedom is not about capricious living without consequence. It is not the absence of laws or rules. You are not limited by those rules, but you cannot ignore them either. Freedom is not what happens when the rules disappear. It is what happens when you disappear. The freedom of enchantment allows you to live before the arbitrary rules of ordinary life without breaking those rules. What does that mean? It means that you live by love, not morality. You live as love, not as some idea about it.

# Power

There is a general presumption that mastery of spiritual or generally miraculous powers is testimony of the highest spiritual achievement. It is not coincidence in a world where most people are—or feel they are—without power that we would regard power as the pinnacle of spirituality, and our deliverance from a disenchanted world. It is clear that the pursuit of power for any reason in any context is more an effort to compensate for the inadequacies of life and self than it is to evolve beyond them. Thus, people seek occult or psychic powers and experiences, mind control, transcendent visions, healing powers, the ability to see auras and read minds, and astral travel. Those with no power always seek the miraculous.

If we regard power as a way to gain wisdom, it is an indirect way at best. The descending path of power is only part of a larger path that includes the ascending path of wisdom. The occult powers of the descending path do not and cannot produce the personal paradigm shift in awareness that the ascending path produces in the event of enlightenment. It is precisely this shift that opens the door to personal evolution. Power alone does not denote evolution. Neither can it solve the problems of ordinary life. If power could solve the tensions of ordinary life, it would have done so long ago. Power is not the path to the enchantment of life on earth.

The direct path of personal and collective evolution is the presumption of love. Let the power you would pursue find you instead, as it will, effortlessly. Allow love to flow through you with ever-increasing force until the intelligence of life dawns within you. You achieve effortlessly what is otherwise a struggle.

All that you seek on any spiritual path, including power, appears in response to your choice to love. You can only pursue power when you have turned from love. There is nothing wrong with power. It is an unavoidable part of life. The issue is the pursuit of power. All good things in life are yours in love.

Descending path traditions are all about the pursuit of and resort to power. Power is darkened by lack of awareness and failure to evolve beyond the need for power. Still, paths of power are filled with often benign, wondrous experiences and insights. But none of it produces evolution or enchantment.

It is difficult to discount personal experiences. But personal and collective evolution do not result from experiences, no matter how profound.

Evolution is a shift in awareness that precedes experience. Evolution by its very nature cannot be experienced.

The pursuit of power is an addiction. It is not by accident that power occurs naturally only after enlightenment. The pursuit of power is just another way to avoid accepting life as it is. If this is your motive, you need a therapist, not a spiritual teacher. For the sake of love, forsake the titillating experiences of power and content yourself with the more subtle energetic play embedded in ordinary experience. That said, if power is a real interest or concern of yours, then by all means pursue it to the fullest prior to committing to love. Until you are finished with all other interests and have converted your life to love, you will be unable to participate in the enchantment of life.

Power is, however, another word for love. To manifest love is to manifest power. Power and love are synonyms only for an original fully human being, an enchanter of life. Be aware that there is power in living without power. The lessons of love must be learned before you come to power. Until you only rely on love, power is a danger to you and to others. You will always find it an enticing way to compensate for what you presume are life's deficiencies in your particular case.

Power is inherent in the universe. You need not pursue it to have it. You live within and experience an energetic play of power every day. If you pursue power, you do so to control it, not to experience it. But if power is the natural result of love, why pursue it? To live in harmony with life, rather than always trying to fix it, is a marvelous way to demonstrate power. The joyful and creative play of life is a demonstration of power. Only a powerful person lives amidst delusion and affirms love.

The desire for power without personal transformation is the goal of all ignorant people. It unavoidably creates unintended consequences that cannot be resolved in a single lifetime (given a lack of awareness and separation from life). The power to enchant life on earth need not be pursued for it will emanate naturally in your life until the world itself is enchanted. Love is how power manifests in ordinary life.

Finally, the power of all higher realms is present here on the physical plane. That power is obvious in every detail of ordinary life. The enchantment of life is everywhere. Power is pursuing us. It has found us. We cannot avoid it. Power is forcing itself upon us. That is the problem. We have more power than we know what to do with. Evolution is not a pastime for misfits and dreamers. It is an essential survival skill. The future belongs to those who evolve.

## The Play of Freedom and Power

Love teaches that the pursuit of power is unnecessary. You are already part of the pattern of forces you want to change. You cannot change that pattern without changing yourself. Those patterns come from your wounds and limitations and those of others. When you evolve, you change these patterns of force. So, the solution for a disenchanted life is evolution, not struggle.

People usually seek power to make some unilateral change that would directly or indirectly benefit them. The problem with enlightenment is that you see these patterns of force and how changing them unilaterally ends up creating unintended consequences.

You cannot control the forces of life without separating from them. You can influence life by freely participating in the play of life with love and intelligence. How? Embrace life until you are enchanted by it, until you *are* the very forces you tried to control. When you embody power, you need not pursue it. Your actions are no longer personal, but express the creative intelligence of life itself.

Freedom does not result from controlling power, but from merging with it. The power you seek is your own power not yet internalized. If you feel powerless, it is because you sense the absence of love.

## How Then Do We Love?

Is there a special technique for evolution? For love? Practices and techniques prevent love. Techniques direct and control your energy. They thwart the deep free-form restructuring of awareness and life evolution demands. Methods and practices rely upon and extend the influence of a given purpose. What you are trying to do is change that purpose. It is the purpose that produces and empowers the methods and practices that extend its influence. Until you change your purpose, all your methods and practices will rely upon and extend the influence of the very purpose you want to change. There is no technique for changing your purpose. How do you change your purpose? How do you change your mind? Who and what do you choose to love?

## The Mind Game of Spiritual Traditions

Experiences are sensitive to technique. The details of every technique create the details of every experience. Enchantment is technique-sensitive. It is antithetical to technique. The only technique for the enchantment of life is love. Technically, love is more of a strategy than an actual technique. But . . .

Techniques solve technical problems. Most problems are called technical because we want them to be amenable to technical solutions for two reasons: 1) They have limited effect. 2) They are nonstructural. They do not demand systemwide change.

When it comes to spiritual matters, then, clearly a technical strategy allows a person to leave most of their life intact while obtaining fascinating experiences. Spiritual practices are meant to be remedies to spiritual ailments, but the practices only produce the experience of a solution, not its reality. Spiritual traditions offer theater that poses as reality. It is all a mind game, a delusion.

Techniques produce results. They are how we achieve goals. But evolution cannot be a goal. Evolution is a restructuring of the context in which goals are achieved, and that structure cannot be known before it occurs. Thus, enchantment resists any and all technical strategies. Spiritual practices distract us from life's evolutionary imperative.

Practicing moral virtues will not produce enchantment either. Moral virtues are moral because they support the status quo, the existing pattern of life. But evolution threatens the status quo with a new possibility. Thus, moral virtues are supposed to be technical solutions to the problems of daily life, but they will not and cannot solve the problems of daily life because they support the pattern of life that is already failing.

It is this incompatibility of evolution and technique that frustrates the average person who wants desperately only to know what to do. But evolution is nonspecific. To induce it, you must relax into your purpose to love. There is no formula for enchantment. To know what to do, you must create solutions, not merely apply them. You must see a relationship between your purpose and the specific need of the moment, and then create a way to bridge that gap in love. The nonspecific strategy of love is ultimately a problem-recognition and problem-solving strategy. It supports a capacity to see the relationship between a present problem and a future goal.

You already are the essence of what you seek. Put it to use. But if you rely on technique, you relieve yourself of responsibility for evolution. That techniques do not produce evolution makes it clear that evolution within spiritual traditions occurs mostly by mistake. (They all rely on various technical means.) Moreover, when and if enlightenment occurs it often is a personal rather than evolutionary enlightenment. Your inner life changes, but not your outer life. Enlightenment within traditions generally results from the failure of technique and expertise, not their success. This is why it happens so rarely. That evolution occurs so rarely within the traditions is also testimony to the technical prowess of traditional practitioners. If they seek merely spiritual experiences, their prowess serves them well. If they seek evolution, however, their prowess only undermines their ability to achieve what they seek.

In the second age of humankind,
The age of the mind and adolescence,
We lived to dominate.

# The Practice of
# Relentless Love

## Experience vs. Evolution

EXPERIENCES DO NOT ALWAYS CREATE CHANGE. Change does not always create experiences. What distinguishes spiritual experience from evolution? Experience changes the *content* of awareness. Evolution changes the *structure* of awareness and life. Evolution does not *increase* experience. It reorganizes experience. Experience adds to knowledge and memories. Evolution does not.

If you seek a spiritual path and practice to improve your quality of life, your experience of life, without altering the *pattern* of your life, then evolution is not for you. The practice of love is a potent process that completely disrupts your inner and outer life. This is because its purpose (its result at least) is evolution, not personal improvement. To evolve is to be a pioneer of the future.

Enchantment is not about improving your quality of life. It is about risking the whole of your life to live on the edge, making an evolutionary leap into the unknown, relying on your wits, your creativity, and a deepened life intelligence to create a new context for human life, to help it achieve its highest possibility. Traditional paths and practitioners generally seek an improved life, not a rugged life of adventure. You can, of course, limit your practice of love and so reduce the depth of change in your life. But if that is what you seek, you are better off in a spiritual tradition.

## Enlightenment vs. Enchantment

Enlightenment is an incomplete reorganization of awareness around intent. It transforms your inner life, not your outer life. Enchantment completely restructures awareness and life around a single intent. It naturally, forcefully seeks outward expression on a global scale. Those people who have had the most profound insights into our human condition and the biggest impact on our history have *died* and been *reborn*. They evolved. They did not merely improve their life. In the past, evolution was assumed to be personally unique, not reproducible. But that is untrue!

The key to producing enchantment on a regular and predictable basis is to understand that no technique can produce it. Your practice is love and nothing else. The free-form reorganization of life and awareness without boundaries occurs spontaneously. Love *is* the practice of enchantment itself. Since love is a process, not a condition, your life can be restructured more than once.

Finally, as love alters your awareness and life, you will be increasingly at odds with and unwilling to participate in the conventions and routines of ordinary life. Every part of your life is being reorganized to create and sustain a different purpose and pattern. Generally, you will find peace only among those of similar purpose. Choose carefully. You cannot reverse evolution.

## Evolutionary Stages

### 1. Unawareness

This is where we begin, a general lack of awareness beyond the thinking self or within it. Awareness is confined primarily to ordinary experience. When there *is* awareness beyond the thinking self, it is regarded as an exclusively psychological or mental event. Only the thinking self is involved here. Evolution is blocked since the original self is not yet part of your purpose.

Those capable of psychic experiences may be called *channels*. Their psychic experiences are perceived to come from beyond the self. Interestingly, such experiences require fairly strong self-boundaries. Without strong boundaries, the experience seems more like an internal dialogue than a voice from beyond.

This stage reflects the limits of ordinary education, which trains the mind by focusing on the *contents* of awareness rather than its structure. Our life is heavily clouded with mind-forms of all sorts—thoughts, emotions, memories, habits, beliefs, attachments, etc.—due largely to the limited and arbitrary result of *mental* training. The thinking self is identified with time, activity, power, objectivity, struggle, limitation, and separateness: the context of ordinary life.

All of this is organized in a way that generates an image (illusion) of self. The self is a mental construct for organizing the contents of awareness. When those contents are transcended, they are also reorganized. The image and definition of self shifts as it is folded into a larger perception of self and reality, the original self.

## THE CULTURE OF ADOLESCENCE

A person is generally ready for such a change during adolescence, which is developmentally the right time. Why then? Formal thought begins in adolescence, but more importantly, one's sense of individuality and separateness emerges in adolescence. This developmental stage begs for a larger context of community in which to mature. Without it, individuality and separateness become the context of personal experience and the limit of identity. The individual learns no way to connect with anyone or anything outside himself.

The biological relationship between child and parent is subject to a natural end as individuality emerges. But what replaces the end of childhood? Nothing. The child is given no context for individuality. As the sense of separateness emerges and is explored, rebellion against all relationships ensues. The child is thrown out of the context of family and abandoned to the vagaries of individuality. Observe any high school culture. What you see are all the neurotic dynamics typical of adult society. The adolescent is functionally an adult at this point.

This is dangerous to any community. Without purpose, individuality must be constrained. Otherwise, it poses a real threat to the stability of adult society. A sense of purpose demands incorporating something beyond the self into one's sense of self. That is the function of the adult community, but the community of modern societies is a cruel joke on adolescents. It cannot and historically has not provided any meaningful context for their development. Modern societies are populated with adults who are in fact functional adolescents. Thus, the adult community cannot provide any guidance for adolescents, except to restrain their emerging individuality by prolonging their adolescence. Teenage years are utterly meaningless for adolescents since the major activity in their life, formal schooling, is entirely generic, irrelevant, and unresponsive to their emerging individuality.

In modern societies, the dissonance of adolescence is viewed not as a call to evolution but as a natural, permanent, and unavoidable condition of life. Indigenous cultures ease people through adolescent turbulence, resolving the conflict between individuality and community, but even still, there is no mechanism for evolution. Rare individuals may evolve, but not the community itself.

During adolescence we begin to see that life generally and our life in particular is awful. Something must change. Given the modern cultural view that suffering and alienation are normal, the only way to end our suffering is to take our adolescent *inner* resources to improve our *outer* life. The result is that life gradually focuses on *addictions*. These include dysfunctional habits of all sorts (not merely drugs) that numb and limit awareness, the accumulation and exploitation of formal power, and the search generally for anything to ease the pain of ordinary life and provide a modicum of control over one's experience of life.

The adolescent insight that *life sucks* is itself remarkable. It is life calling us to evolve. But since adolescents cannot act on their own behalf, and since the culture says there is nothing to do with this insight but to tough it out, we do not take meaningful steps toward evolution until well past adolescence, if we take steps at all.

During adolescence, we resist the power of life, sensing a need to prevent things from getting any worse. We try to direct or control the events and experiences of our life. We live in a confusion of self-initiated goals and methods. We compete with others for the right to live well. But at some point the adolescent insight recurs and if we are ready for the adventure, the neurotic, limited, imperfect, struggling and suffering-bound existence of adolescent life ends in the *search*.

THE SEARCH

This is a transitional phase, a search for answers—some asked, most not. The search is an adventure. You come to know all the possible remedies for your suffering. Usually, the search involves a shift from manipulating others to get what you want to manipulating yourself (change induced through internal self-coercion or *discipline*).

The search often involves psychological self-confrontation, where you become gradually and reluctantly self-aware. Such self-awareness is most often not sought, but simply the unintended result of the search for power and control. Such a search may manifest as an interest in, and efforts to master, *feminine* powers (paganism). Searching for power and control is fascinating and addictive. It alters ordinary experience and distracts you from deeper evolutionary demands. But you are only faced with a more interesting version of life, filled with the same unsolved problems. It does not work. It cannot work. Problems persist individually and collectively, because they are *systemic*—structural not technical. The entire pattern and nature of the thinking self and ordinary life is generating the problems that never go away, which we must solve again and again.

Finally, or perhaps not, the most sophisticated way to avoid life, the most subtle form of power and control, appears on the horizon of your search: mystical spirituality. Gradually, the pursuit of power is seen as just another form of personal greed. So the seeker moves on to paths of mystical insight and wisdom. But this is still only another way to play the same tune of need and greed. You still pursue various goals as a remedy for a felt dilemma of personal suffering and struggling. But there is the additional bonus of entertaining mystical visions and insights!

The various traditions (pagan and mystic) often regale the seeker with trappings much like a mystical theme park. Theater has a large role in all traditions because, ultimately, life is only collective, interactive, impromptu theater. But the adolescent sensibilities of the seeker are not ready to create such theater. Rather, the seeker is entranced by it—a child in a candy store. The seeker thinks she has at last found the true form of life because it is so far removed from the ordinary. The seeker believes she has moved beyond forms of self-remedy and consolation. But it is no different than a well decorated movie theater.

## 2. Enlightenment

There is a lot of change to occur between the search and enlightenment, but until the moment of enlightenment, the search continues. The motivational shift from fear and inner tension to love occurs in four phases: conversion, enlightenment, realization, and enchantment. Conversion is a conscious commitment to love, allowing love to bring your life into congruence with love. It is a clear acknowledgement of a change in purpose. The energetic and functional effect of conversion is a deliberate, but unstable, connection between the thinking self and the original self.

That change of purpose naturally generates problem-solving insights and practices. For instance, Original Meditation—a formal practice of love as an exclusively internal process—develops spontaneously in response to brainstem impulses.

Original Meditation leads quickly to the enlightenment of the mind. The thinking self is the first casualty of love because that is where the most healing is required. Until the mind is healed at least minimally, the remaining evolutionary process cannot proceed. Enlightenment is a transforming event that stabilizes the connection between the two selves. The result is insight, wisdom, a functional rewiring of the neo-cortex.

Enlightenment increases your awareness of the depth of your suffering and its causes (fear) and brings a certain release from its more onerous manifestations. But the fear at the root of suffering remains largely untouched. So, enlightenment is insufficient for enchantment. Enlightenment unleashes the wisdom that allows you to pursue learning with more precision and sophistication, more sincerity and enthusiasm. But in the end, enlightenment has only one thing to teach you: you must evolve beyond wisdom.

In many ways, enlightenment leaves you unsatisfied. There is a recognition that something is still not over. Of course, evolution is never over, but that is not it. When the dust of enlightenment settles, there is a deep knowing that something you thought, expected, and hoped would be over, isn't. This insight does not come immediately on the heels of enlightenment. You can be so entranced with your wisdom and other dramatic changes, it may be years before you recognize that suffering is still hanging around. The game is not yet over if you want to end suffering. This is a profound disillusionment: enlightenment cannot end suffering.

The search taints the process of enlightenment. You may be content with your ignorance. You may be acutely aware of it as you come to enlightenment. But suffering still prompts you to stay with your personal regime and disciplines of practice. You know the value of love, but you feel pressured to continue through thick and thin by the fact of your continuing suffering.

And quite correctly. Your work is not complete. After enlightenment, you still relate to the world (and even your self) through the prism of your mind and wisdom. You still identify with the mind even when you know you are not your mind. Brain functions are not yet fully merged. You cannot live what you know. You see the contradictions of the search, but they remain.

Enlightenment also does not answer a fundamental question: What do I do now? Indeed, is there *anything* to do after enlightenment? It is disingenuous to say enjoy your life. How do you meet life's demands from an enlightened perspective without betraying the sensibilities that you struggled to achieve? What form should your life take? Perhaps the answer is just to resume your life as it was before enlightenment. If your enlightenment occurs within a spiritual tradition, the answer is provided by the tradition. A place is provided for masters of the tradition free of the conventional demands and travails of life. In this context, the perception of suffering is assuaged, if not overcome. Still, enlightenment cannot tell you what to do *after* enlightenment. It modifies the search, but does not end it. The root of suffering, after all, is in inhibitions imposed on the brainstem. Enlightenment transforms the neo-cortex. There is still a long way to go.

## 3. Realization

So, the search continues beyond enlightenment. The insights of enlightenment bring an ever-maturing view of your life and what it demands of you, and all of us. But finally, the third stage is reached: realization, the enlightenment of the *heart* (mid-brain).

On reflection, you realize your attachment to wisdom and insight. You notice your habit of relating to the world through your mind and insights. Your wisdom has become a substitute for yourself, a shield against the unrelenting, unaware, unsympathetic demands of conventional life. You have lived aloof from life. You have avoided it! (Oh no!)

The tendency to avoid life after enlightenment is true of all who are enlightened, but it is easier to rationalize when you are in a tradition where you are venerated and well thought of. In a conventional life, your sensibilities and insights are anomalous, disruptive. Conventional life organizes around sensibilities, values, and goals at odds with your own. Indeed, the energy of your presence alone is often enough to put other people on notice about you.

THE EXPERIENCE OF REALIZATION

Realization is the *mind* spontaneously *sinking* into the *heart* (the neo-cortex connecting to the mid-brain). You feel, quite literally, as if the floor of reality has just vanished. You *fall*, as in a dream, into an abyss, frightening only in that it is unexpected. The original self begins emerging with self-awareness. The question of enlightenment (what do I do?) is now self-evident. You are, always have been, always will be, living in the appropriate form because there is none. The form your life will take results from creative play between you and the rest of life. This is an insight into the upcoming transformation of enchantment.

There is a deep sensation of self-acceptance, of reality without boundaries. Personal suffering ends. There is also a sense that you have just begun. You now know that you are and always have been in the proper place, doing the proper thing in the world. You now have no focus as you sink into and break out of all boundaries and forms. You come to know intuitively, not intellectually, that you are complete, perfect, whole, infinite, as you are. You no longer identify with activity and limitation. You know your original self as complete and perfect. You realize there is nothing more to do, no more forms of perfection. There is only what is, which is already perfect.

The self is now fully a paradox. You have *died*, yet you survive and thrive in a form, as a person, which is you and yet is *more* than you. Beyond this moment is the infinite ever. And so here ends ignorance, avoidance, motivation, and suffering. You pass beyond the separateness of the two selves into unity with the energetic realm of the Primordial Spirit, eternity, infinity. All other insights, possibilities, experiences, powers, are second to this. The entire structure of your existence is radically undone, unmade, uncreated. You enter into the world of your prior existence as an entirely new being. You have died in the energetic fires of the Primordial Spirit and been reborn in the mythic realm. The locale of your identity has moved. Your life slowly becomes impersonal, mythic. You notice the broad, archetypal organizing energies that give structure and direction to the life at all levels. You feel their presence and movement in you.

The mind is further transformed. It is no longer a channel for light, but light itself. You have moved from being a small part of life to being the whole of life. You are now both fully finite *and* infinite. You were a mere channel for life. Now you are the Original Primordial Self. Remember, the brainstem is in constant mystic union with all realms. As attention moves to the brainstem, self-awareness is lost. You experience unmitigated wholeness. You swoon in the energies of life.

## 4. Enchantment: The Transformation of Life on Earth

After realization, you are different. You have been evolving, but until now it was largely a personal, internal process with localized and limited results. Not anymore. You were not like others before. Now you are *really* not like others. It is all very subtle still, nothing overt at first, but palpable nonetheless. You are no longer congruent with conventional life. If you have no tradition to protect you and justify your existence, you must work to fit into the world of human concerns, more so now than before. But the more you try, the worse things get.

Interestingly, this serves a useful purpose. The suffering of others increasingly becomes your own. *You* are not suffering, but suffering is there, in awareness. You share the suffering of others, silently. For anyone else, this would be an unbearable burden. Realization ended *you* and all the problems of you. There is no more you. There is only the body and your problems are all quite small, literal. The suffering you sense comes almost as relief. There is something to do! You are drawn into solving the problem of suffering on a larger scale. Creative problem-solving and compassion work together as you delve into the details of untying this existential knot. The idea that no one is truly happy until everyone is happy is now personally and literally true.

You see that personal suffering is not the result of personal activity only. It also has roots in *collective* activity! You cannot be an island of nonsuffering amidst the general tragedy of life. The collective activity and condition of the world haunts your awareness and experience at every level, in every moment. Personal suffering has roots in how we organize our lives. Personal and collective suffering is embedded in and sustained by cultural, political, and economic institutions and processes. These are active sources of suffering. Of course, those institutions and processes express the suffering and limitations of those who created them and continue to support them. It is a global dance of suffering and everyone knows the steps.

Suffering, then, is not merely a personal psychological event. It is *political* as well. Life does not leave you alone. And you cannot leave life alone either. The problem of conventional life must be solved. Evolution now has purpose, and a champion.

The formerly *personal* process of evolution is now interpersonal, literal, and global. Until now, it focused on self-remediation and healing. With the union of the two selves, you live an entirely new human possibility. In a way, your evolution is just beginning. Your life is no longer your own. You are now a goad to the evolution of others. Welcome to the future.

# Spiritual Experiences

We all face the ongoing problem of how to relate to and understand experiences, especially spiritual experiences. It is the tendency to distinguish spiritual from ordinary experiences that prevents enchantment. We presume one experience is more significant than another, so we seek them out. By making such distinctions, we avoid the directness and simplicity of enchantment.

Spiritual practices focus attention on *aspects* of reality. Awareness of these aspects becomes a spiritual experience. Our search for a spirit-based life appears to be bearing fruit. But is it really? Experiences have no inherent significance, most especially no spiritual significance. The meaning of an experience rests with you. For instance, when you *learn a lesson* from an experience, you bring that lesson *to* the experience. When you are ready, *any* experience can trigger learning.

Your habits of attention express your purpose and dispose you to certain perceptual habits. The evolutionary significance of an experience is that it reflects, and so exposes, the illusions and limits of the thinking self (provided you want to notice). All experiences contain lessons and value. If you want to know if your efforts are bearing fruit, look to the love expressed in your life.

## An Awareness Exercise
On some paths, you are given certain practices that create certain experiences when you have achieved a certain proficiency or understanding or shifted to a certain level in consciousness. All of this is focus-pocus. Evolutionary lessons are energetic. The meaning of an experience is its impact on your life. Your body registers the meaning of every lesson directly and immediately. There is no guesswork here. By the time you are aware of something, its meaning has been felt, its lesson absorbed. However, you may also want to do the following exercises.

### EXERCISE ONE, CORE
Observe any experience. Notice your thoughts, feelings, and body sensations. Whatever impressions or sensations come to mind without effort are the meaning of the experience. If you can make sense out of these impressions, fine. If not, do not worry. Evolutionary lessons are learned spontaneously, in the body. You will see the lesson everywhere when you are

learning it, until you are changed by it. If you miss the lesson in one experience, it will show up in another.

EXERCISE ONE, COMPLETE

To use experiences for spiritual evolution: 1) Observe the experience. Acknowledge that any lesson can be learned from any experience. 2) Notice the apparent insight or feeling that comes to mind easily, if any. 3) Accept the experience. Understand it has no ultimate meaning. 4) Release the experience and meaning. Do not engage in mental or emotional speculation or judgment. Again, you need not understand an experience for it to benefit your healing and learning.

## Using Experiences to Evolve

Experiences stimulate spontaneous changes in the body. You might notice thoughts connected to deep feelings as this occurs. Give yourself to these moments. Be there with whatever is going on and let it continue until it comes to a natural endpoint. You need not know or do anything for these changes to occur, other than to let it happen. Your purpose, the body's intent, and your faith (relaxation) give permission for evolution to proceed. No further permission is required.

It is difficult to break the habit of valuing certain experiences as proof that your choice to love is working. This inhibits the process. Trust your body and your choice. This makes you available to more varied energetic influences and speeds up the process of evolution.

## Overcoming the Fear of Evolution

Goals inhibit evolution. They reinforce energetic habits you want to overcome. Like what? First, goals can only lead to desired results *within* an organized system. In disorganized systems, a goal is at best an experiment. You are never quite sure what will happen when you have no organized way to achieve a goal. But evolution allows a *new* organizational pattern or habit to emerge. Evolution *is* an experiment, for real. You are relaxing and letting your body adapt to life on an energetic level. Second, goals seek achievement, not evolution. Goals work when there is nothing to learn. Your best strategy for evolution and learning is to jump into the infinite culture of life, allow for completely free interaction, and let the evolution begin!

Since evolution is an unpredictable experiment, all you can do is accept the results you get and regard them as benign. Anything you recognize as proof of the need to end the experiment only reflects your fears more than your wisdom. You cannot know if the evolutionary experiment is succeeding or failing. You must trust it is succeeding. If you believe the experiment is failing, the experiment stops and so does evolution. All that is left is a life of self-concern.

For love to produce evolution, it must have no boundaries. It must be deep love. It must serve no purpose. It is not a way to get something. Love is a way of life, a strategy of embracing life without fear or limit. Love is a way to be, not a way to achieve. Life is best lived in its original and simplest form: love. The less we love life, the less benign is our experience of it. Love is the original blueprint of human life. To experience it, your inner life must return to its original form. Love is the only strategy that proactively simplifies life so we experience it as enchanted.

## Love Promotes Intelligence

Traditional paths offer practices to awaken the mind from the darkness of illusion. NOT! In love, there is no darkness. Everything is accepted. Nothing is rejected. Love's lack of structure can be a shortcoming, but it is really its strength. The emphasis on purpose, rather than practices, forces you to *creatively* respond to life while remaining true to the purpose of love. This is more demanding than a do-it-by-the-numbers path. Love promotes creative intelligence, not ritual.

## Love Is Preemptive Awareness

Love is *preemptive* awareness and understanding. Love is trusting life *before* you are aware of what you are trusting and understanding that life is benign *before* you can notice it. If you withhold love because you do not understand what could happen, then love will elude you. You will have only your fears. Understanding cannot come before love, or else you would not need it.

## The Heart Is Never Blind

Love is never blind. But *you* can be blind. So, trust your body. *Then* wonder. *Then* doubt. *Then* question. *Then* suspect the sincerity of your choice. Never take love for granted. Trust, but verify! Again, love is not a do-it-by-the-numbers process. Love first, relentlessly. *Then* review your intention, your faith, your love, your understanding, or experience, or *you will* be blind.

## Making Love True

By the time you notice what is going on in love, everything has already happened. This is not a way to control what you do, only a way to understand what you have done. What good is that? Awareness of what you have done changes what you do next. It changes who you are. So, let us suppose you think your purpose is love, but it isn't. You don't know that yet, so you act in good faith and discover, to your dismay, that what you are doing is *not* love. This after-the-fact awareness alters what you do in the following moment, and so you move toward love. This is basic learning theory. Now let us take the same situation, with a twist: You think your intention is love, but it isn't. You don't know that yet, so you act in good faith and discover that what you are doing is not love. Here is the twist: there is no dismay! You notice, but without concern. This is good, right? No. The lack of dismay means your choice to love is insincere. The *dismay* is the pain of unrequited love. The dismay of failed love moves you toward love.

## The Sacred Theater of Unrequited Love

This intrapersonal theater of unrequited love also occurs as interpersonal sacred theater (the transformational drama of enchantment). Sacred theater demands a higher level of energetic maturity than engaging the process alone because it is possible to misinterpret the interaction and miss the evolutionary opportunity it offers. When you interact in good faith of your choice to love with someone familiar with the process, you may discover your interaction is not as loving as you would like. You experience unrequited love. You get back what you think you don't deserve. Of course, you are not offering what you think you are. You do not get love because you do not offer it. Of course, that much honesty may be unwanted. If so, then your choice to love is insincere. It is only when you feel dismay, rather than anger and rejection, that your choice to love is sincere. Anger occurs when you think other people are expressing *themselves* rather than reflecting *you*. What is really going on? You cannot know. It is a waste of time to parse out fault. Whether it is you or them, your response must be the same: love. As you turn the other cheek, you internalize the energy of unrequited love. The energy moves from anger (about what *they* did) to dismay (about what *you* did): evolution!

## To Love Is to Learn

How do you know you are doing it right? Find out for yourself. Be aware. Notice. Don't follow some theory or practice. Such questions or doubts may arise because success often seems like failure. (Oh, great! Isn't this hard enough already?). Often we doubt we are succeeding or simply do not know how to proceed. Confusion about our choices, past and future, all reflect a normal learning curve, which for evolution is always straight up. You learn something when there is an energy shift in the body. You literally become a different person. This new pattern, this new you, encounters the challenges of life in love for the first time. Every instance of love is the first.

## The Mind Is Always Blind

This means we never learn from our mistakes. (What? It gets worse?). We are not supposed to learn from our mistakes. We are supposed to change from them. What we learn intellectually does not help us practice love. In each moment, we abandon what we know in favor of facing the moment naively, in love. Our knowledge cannot help us predict or control the results of our efforts. Past experience does not help us recognize the present moment, implicitly telling us how to proceed. We approach each moment innocently, without a past. Thus we maximize the energetic impact of each moment and minimize the obstructing effects of prior knowledge. This is why and how real change always comes as such a surprise. You cannot see it coming.

This means we live each moment blind, in trust, as a child with no past, ahead of the moment of self-awareness. In effect, we blurt out our lives with complete abandon. This is a natural form of confession and healing catharsis. We then notice what we do after the fact and that awareness forms a natural context for the next moment. And so we evolve. This is already going on. You are, right now, living before you are aware of what you are doing. The body forces us all into love. We are embedded in life before we know it. So, do you give in to love, or resist it?

## Converting from Experience

There comes a time when our inner life screams for us to recognize that our efforts to perfect our life have failed. If you are lucky, you give up the struggle and sink into love. You can love only when you live in life rather than an *experience* of life. Love abides only in the moment *before* experience. There is the simplicity of only love. There is the moment of enchantment.

Your body takes your mind by the hand and leads it into life. Your body renders you defenseless in life, and so facilitates your evolution. You are always being undone by the intent of your body to love. The mind can only inhibit evolution. Believe nothing. Accept everything. It is your direct and unmitigated encounter with life that matters, only that.

When you accept life directly, there is love, not knowledge. There can be no knowledge. The mind is not yet present. This way, the present precedes and overwhelms the past (your history, knowledge). Later, insight may arise in response to this encounter. Abandon this. After a while, you notice a pattern emerging from these encounters. Life has created something in you while you were busy embracing it in trust. Let go of whatever you notice and return to the first moment of love. Whatever meaning it has for you, it is just a reflection distracting you from the play of life in love. Quickly, or you will miss the enchantment of *this* moment! Embrace this moment. Stop observing. Stop believing what you experience. Relax, and fall into love.

## The Perfection of Imperfection

To be *perfect* is to be whole, at ease with imperfection and change. Perfection is living in limits without being limited, being perfectly human without effort. Perfection is not necessary for evolution, nor the result of it. Suffering and struggling, laughter and tears, all come and go. It is all part of a life that excludes nothing. The trick is not to focus on experience, but on intention.

How do we prevent mistakes? An enchanted life is filled with mistakes. Evolution is a course of events you do not like (i.e., mistakes) that create a possibility you did not anticipate. Mistakes generate learning: walking is a by-product of falling down. Perhaps you think perfection is about knowing. In love you never know. You are new to the moment, learning, never knowing. There are lots of times you think you know. Then you wonder why an expectation was not met, a goal not achieved. You shrug it off, but it happens again. You pay more attention. Still nothing. You become confused. You are doing what you always have, but something is wrong.

Evolution. Dilemma and crisis arise as old patterns give way to new. Change is here. You become frustrated with details you did not notice before, and that did not matter. We try to hurry through this part. No one likes crisis. But that is the reason for love. Do not try to fix your life. Ending the crisis interferes with evolution. Live in the confusion. It will resolve itself. It will.

We cannot prevent mistakes. If we try, we will come to view human life as tainted and unjust. Life is not a race to win a perfection contest. Life is already and always perfect. We only perceive imperfection. There is nothing wrong with you, or the world. Imperfection is a failure to perceive perfection because you focus on what you dislike. We are perfect and most human in love.

## Impulse Control

To be perfectly human is to live in the original moment of love's intent. That does not mean you give in to impulses! That is one way to find your original self, but it also creates hardships and wounds for yourself and others. Acting on impulse is not the same as trusting your instincts. Impulses are unloved parts of yourself. Acting on them is neurotic and self-absorbed. It is just a way to relieve the creative tension of evolution. Still, how can you distinguish impulse from love? If you live your life in the moment *before* awareness and self-control, how can you avoid neurotic impulses? (Think you've got me now, don't you?). Live your life internally, before it is enacted.

Remember the four moments of intention, faith, attention, and action? Impulses appear in the moment of attention, when *you* appear. To avoid acting out neurotic impulses, live the first two moments in trust. Notice the impulses. Then, in the moment of action, relax and choose not to act them out. You can intervene in the moment before action without compromising the authenticity of the prior moments. All that matters is that the impulses come to awareness. Once they do, relax and so convert their energy. As you become aware, your life internalizes, but without the self-control or suppression that distorts your inner life. Your inner life becomes honest and healthy. Your outer life becomes stable, less prone to dramatic and impulsive fluctuations. Slow down and live each moment. Give yourself time to notice the difference between love and impulse. Relax. Let evolution rage within you. Do not externalize your life drama. As evolution internalizes, the outward drama subsides. Eventually, your life must be shared with others, but only *after* you learn how not to involve others in your drama, and only they know how not to succumb to it.

# Justice: The Call to Heal

The idea of karma is about life's justice. It refers to the law of cause and effect: every action has an effect. We act in all realms (physical, personal, mythic, intentional). We generate effects in those realms. A corollary of karma is reincarnation—also about life's justice. Here, unlearned *lessons* (limiting energetic patterns) accumulate from one life to the next. Reincarnation and karma suggest we cannot escape the effects of our actions even in death.

What kind of effects are we talking about? Every moment is four moments that occur all at once in each realm (energetic, mythic, psychological, and physical). A complete moment is when all parts of a moment are congruent or in harmony with each other. A moment is incomplete, then, when any of it is unloved or unlived. Only when a moment is fully loved is it complete. Karma is the accumulation of unloved moments. Each such moment is a wound in the soul (personal energetic field). So, whatever is unloved in our lives haunts us until we complete or heal that moment. Evolution occurs as we complete or love all of our unloved moments.

## No Atonement

Karma, then, is not about punishment, but love and the price of not loving. Karma is a call to life in the fullest sense. We must love completely, not partly or mostly. Life does not forgive us our failure to love. There is nothing to forgive. There is only the result of our actions. The price of not loving is the absence of love in our life. *There* is justice: a world that mirrors our inner life.

Justice does not demand we be punished for not loving. It does not even demand we change. Life simply reflects our choices and habits. We decide if we want to change the reflection. If so, we need only love fully, in each of our moments. And, oh yes, suffering is not the result of past unloved moments. It results from the failure to love in this moment. It is not the past that haunts us. It is our present. Finally, the unintended consequences of an act are not really consequences, but completions—the return of unloved portions of a moment. Embrace them and heal.

## Evolutionary Healing

Everything we experience, everything that is true of us, is an energy pattern that exists in and around the body. Everything affects our energy field: what we do, what others do, what we fail to do, what others fail to do. Ill health occurs as unloved moments accumulate. These moments accumulate because they are not free of us until we complete them. As these moments heal, we experience progressive enlightenments. When we are healed, we experience enchantment. Healing, learning, and evolution are all synonyms.

The enchantment of life on earth, then, proceeds from one individual to another until we are all healed in love.

Evolutionary healing requires *purification* and *communion*, the core strategies of mysticism and paganism respectively. *Purification* is getting rid of what you don't need. *Communion* is getting what you do need. But neither strategy is complete by itself. Evolutionary healing requires the integration of both strategies.

*Purification* begins with your choice to love. As you choose only love, everything that is incompatible with love is released. *Communion* begins as you practice only love and the energies you embrace disrupt your current energy pattern. These energies must align themselves with the only template available: the body's intent to love. Thus, the process of communion is healing and empowering. The strategies of purification and communion are archetypal processes. No healing method does anything more or less than remove or integrate energies.

## The Healing Theater of Enchantment

Sacred theater is an interactive drama or play (depending on how grim you are) that occurs when people interact within a mutually held purpose of respect and love. Ever tell a joke or tease someone who did not find it funny because they did not know you well enough to know you were kidding? The context of an exchange changes its effect. Love is the only context where deep healing can occur. Such healing does not require a master and a disciple. It only requires two people interacting in love. In love, each person is more deeply affected by their interaction than they would be in any other context. In love, every interaction is mutually healing. In love, life becomes sacred theater. In love, life becomes a spiritual path of evolutionary healing. In love, life becomes a *mythic play*, an interaction of mythic forces. Life is no longer merely personal.

## Seeing the Mythic Realm

We limit the power of a moment when we relate to it as merely literal or personal. So, increase the healing and evolutionary power in each moment by allowing each moment to be mythic as well as literal. Look for how each moment relates to your choice to love. Assume all events conspire to further your purpose in life. Notice how. Describe events in nonspecific terms. Use similes, analogies, metaphors, images. Make comparisons between literal events and experiences and a way to describe them that is imaginative, poetic. This book is filled with metaphors. Sacred theater is a metaphoric reference to a healing process. Healing is a metaphor for change, as is evolution. As you try to describe events and experiences without referencing their specific details, you will find yourself relying on metaphors and mythic language.

In sacred theater, your life is not a merely personal drama. It is sacred or mythic theater. Metaphors help us see the link between the literal and the mythic realms. Think how to describe the role or function an event or person plays in your life. As you do, you accept even unwanted or unpleasant events, people and experiences as part of your healing theater, your evolutionary path. Life is transformative when it is mythic.

## Breathing Through Your Wounds

Evolution is healing the incompleteness of your life. To heal your wounds, embrace the wholeness of life in this moment, relax, and breathe (literally and metaphorically) the fullness of life into it. Breathe slow and deep. Endure the pain of your wounds. That is how they will heal. As you do, your life simplifies. Healing reduces the conflicting energies in your life and so simplifies your life. Love all that is untouched, unloved.

## The Play of Justice

We value privacy. We want to keep the awkwardness of our inner life unseen. But nothing about our inner life is unseen, really. Everyone sees everything, even if not consciously. We intuit each other's wounds. And we often reject others in response to our intuitions. When that happens, we create an incomplete moment—for ourselves.

This reactive drama could continue indefinitely, all parties feeling and acting justified, self-righteous. But, we only make life more complicated for each other and ourselves. Eventually, the sheer mass of unrequited love overwhelms us. So, despite how egregiously treated we were, we must internalize our reactions and forgive. Embrace the moment. Embrace each other Continue on your way in love and kindness. Or life can only be a drama of unrequited love.

Our lives are always the result of choices we make *now*. We bring the incompleteness of our past forward into the present by failing to complete those moments now. It is that choice that is problematic. The past and the present must be healed by being completely lived, now. Love the past and the present now, or our lives will be haunted until we do.

## Helping Others

Evolution requires we embrace our pain. Few people have the fortitude for that. Still, if we do, we free the energy of our pain and can then claim it as creative power. To heal is to empower. This is how evolution occurs. We heal by embracing our pain. Others heal by embracing *their* pain. A need to help others end their pain speaks to self-concern and self-obsession. You are not ending their pain. You are ending your own.

The cause of failure to love is not something we can fix for others. Ultimately, we can only heal ourselves. We can only help others heal themselves. It is not our skill that heals others. It is their choice to love. To heal others, help them endure and embrace their suffering until it heals.

Every humane being wants to spare others pain, suffering, struggling. However, life is an energetic system that reflects our choices. To heal another is to overwhelm their choices. So, can we help? Should we help? Living your life in love without compromise helps others do the same. However, others may interpret your willingness to tolerate their pain as a lack of love. (We now return to the sacred theater of unrequited love). They are offended. By implying their suffering is a choice, you threaten the status quo. You encourage them to choose again.

# The Enchanted Life

Ours is a world of oppositional relations: up and down, spirit and matter. The world we think we live in is full of conflict, separation. It is a world of no-love. But our original enchanted life is rooted in the intent to love. Here there are no oppositional relationships. Imagine how you would live in the world if you had no ideas about it, no concepts to structure awareness, no knowledge to guide actions. You would have a naïve relationship to the world. You would live ahead of your fears. Life would be simple, direct, powerful, joyful.

Enchantment is about life as few people actually live it: a single reality unified by the singular intent to love. It is a life that is enthusiastic yet peaceful, exuberant yet quiet. There is a primal zest that directly expresses your trust in life's goodness. A baby trusts its mother because the baby does not experience itself as separate. So too, an original human being, an enchanter of life, trusts and has no fear of life. How can the left hand fear the right hand?

## We Have Always Been Enchanters

A life lived in the original moment is immediate. Nothing intervenes between cause and effect. It is a direct experience of life. An enchanted life is therefore *intimate*. The means for such a life is at hand, in your brain. We are quite literally hard-wired for love. We have assumed, or been told, such possibilities were for only the few, or for only the one. But the possibility of enchantment is true of all of us, in our brain. The time has come to try once again.

The original self functions before and without boundaries or barriers, without a net. Everything in life affects you as a result. You belong to life. You are affected by every event, vibration, every nuance in life. You are not always aware of it, but life is living you.

## Change Your Relationships, Not Your Actions

When you pursue a traditional spiritual path, you expect to alter your activities. This focus on spiritual *form* prolongs your path and delays enchantment. To believe there is a uniquely spiritual habit of life is only another illusion to overcome. You pursue enchantment to alter your *relationships*, not your activities, in life. The goad to enchantment is not unsatisfactory activities, but unsatisfactory relationships. Activities cannot alter your relationship to life, but relationships are the context for all your activities. Context controls actions.

## The Burden of Enchantment

When your life is mythic, enchanted, other people intuit your energy as a challenge to their reality. And your experience of *their* energy field challenges your reality. Enchantment enforces an evolutionary imperative for everyone. The life of an original human being is not a frivolous utopia of narcissistic pleasure, or an escape from ignorance or pettiness. It is a courageous, loving, joyful embrace of life's possibilities, knowing that in that embrace, life is healed, made whole, freed. This is the life of one who enchants life into wholeness and health. It is a life not to be regarded lightly. The enchantment of life on earth cannot manifest until you are strong enough to accept its burdens. An enchanted life is not a vacation from life, but it is a life of love.

## Deep Community

Community is the social form of communion—giving, receiving, learning, teaching, sharing—the full play of opposites in essential harmony. It is a collective and deep embrace of life in love. In deep community, members function as a single whole, not a collection of merely cooperating individuals. It is not a network of organized relationships. Rather, each member functions consciously in the original moment of love, before all other moments. Each member is directly connected with, and an extension of, the others. The experience or action of each affects them all.

## Social Justice

The only possible context for evolution is freedom. This has decided social and political implications beyond the scope of this book. Still, it is important to note that personal freedom and social justice are not the norm in the world. Thus, personal evolution must be internalized because a group's energy is always diverted to healing its most wounded members if you don't.

Evolutionary learning and healing must become the context, not the content, of any group process. Otherwise, group process devolves into conflicting personal wounds and needs. Not only is this simply no fun, it slows down personal evolution. It is best to internalize the process before moving into a group process. Thus, the group only deals with group issues, not personal issues. If this can be done, the group and the individual support their mutual evolution.

Personal evolution demands social evolution: global political and economic change rooted in the emergence of a Collective Infinite Self. Individuals are drawn to any social context congruent with their purpose. Most groups reflect the neurotic and limiting presumptions of their members. When group dynamics are rooted in personal evolution, however, individuals create a collective original self that forms an intuitive context (sacred theater) for personal interactions. Sacred theater challenges us to personal evolution and facilitates evolution both inside and outside the group. This is the promise and mechanism for the enchantment of life. For now, we must make our peace with our social context, or the energy of evolution will be consumed in conflict.

## Privacy

We are typically more concerned about the privacy of our inner life than our outer life. Outer life is public. Inner life is personal, private. In deep community, that polarity is reversed. Your inner life is unavoidably shared because fully aware and connected community members notice. Privacy is about separateness, which ends naturally in deep community. On the other hand, the conventional effort to organize public life for the sake of social order is unnecessary. The group's public life has no apparent outward organization because it is managed inwardly through deep communion. Rules and laws become important only as you move out of deep communion.

In deep communion, everyone has a shared or common inner life. Differences are processed personally as part of your core responsibility to the group. That part of you which is uniquely your own is still present, but purified and restructured in love, so it does not separate you from life or others. Each person is utterly transparent to all. Each person enters deep community as their capacity for communion allows. You participate as you internalize your private life.

## Social Etiquette

Deep community is possible and should be attempted only after members succumb fully to love and are purified in its fires. Otherwise, personal relationships are in endless turmoil. In deep community, the personal and social context of fear, criticism, and judgment gives way to mutual acceptance and healing. The outward community reflects the inner life of its members. Thus, the need for social formalities (etiquette) to grease the wheels of social interaction is absent. The mutual honesty required for deep healing trumps the inherent dishonesty of social etiquette. Members internalize rather than socialize their inner process. As your inner life is healed, it becomes more transparent. You are able to move into deep community easily.

Social etiquette is a form of self-control that encourages you to ignore or hide your inner life while giving the outward appearance of community or relationship. Our inner life is the demon we all try to hide in relationships. Etiquette is how we hide our inner life and politely ignore the inner life of others. We become robots, units of polite social interaction, designed to confirm the illusion of harmony where none exists. But etiquette is irrelevant, unnecessary, intrusive in a loving environment. Community is not therapy. It is what arises naturally after therapy is over. The drama of personal evolution need not become the object or content of community. Social interactions can be inherently healing, but only as you succumb to the intent to love.

By emphasizing transparency more than etiquette, the idea that human beings are essentially benign is put to the test. It is the opposite presumption and our lack of inner self-mastery that lead us all to recoil from the idea of a world without etiquette or privacy. But in a loving world, etiquette is seen for what it really is—a social lie that encourages personal and social stagnation.

Of course, honesty is just a beginning. It is a process, not an outcome. It only opens the door to love. Do not engage in interpersonal honesty before you have mastered intrapersonal honesty. Until you can internalize the process of unrequited love, your contributions to a group can and will only express unresolved issues. This mutuality of ignorance is not therapeutic. Evolution moves from inside to outside, not the other way around. Your inner life must evolve before your outer life can. You cannot be in community before you are a whole individual.

## Evolution: Relax and Restructure

The process of personal evolution is *relax* and *restructure*. *Relax* concern and control of your life. Loosen the energetic bonds that maintain your current habit of life. Then let the original self *restructure* your life in love. Personal evolution is a phasing between these two activities: relax and restructure. Love and embrace your life, then trust your body to transform it. This simple process must be repeated again and again until it is how you live. Relaxing and restructuring is how we make each moment complete. It involves: 1) Intent (intentional realm), making the body's intent to love your own. 2) Faith (mythic realm), trusting the body's intent to love. 3) Attention (personal realm), relaxing and noticing activity in all realms. 4) Action (physical realm), acting in harmony with the body's intent.

Original Meditation combines these actions into one. It is not the practice of these actions, but the practice of love that includes these actions. As you practice, your life transforms in all realms because each moment of practice is a complete moment (a congruent act in all realms).

Leveraging evolution through activity doesn't work. Activity occurs too late in the moment for evolution. Experience is not indicative of evolution. You will not find evolution in the moment of experience (awareness or action), but only in the moment of origination and intent. Only intuition can testify to evolution. Change is not evolution. The process works when you worry less about doing things right and more about what you are learning. Evolution does not result from a conventional cause-effect formula. You are learning the inherent magic of life, which is rooted in awareness and love. The only stable place in your life will be your purpose. This can be disconcerting and confusing. It is unlike anything you have ever tried. If this seems a bit much for you, but you are not daunted by it, find someone familiar enough with the process to engage you in it. Do not go to someone who will teach you. Go to someone who will join you, in love.

## The Process of Community

What is the purpose of deep community? The short answer is there is no purpose. The question is wrong. Deep community does not form around a purpose, but a process: love. The purpose of love is to live together in love, to explore and manifest the possibilities of human life in love, to create and enjoy the play of life. In love, lots of purposes can be served. You might think deep community is about evolution, healing, creativity. Those result from deep community. They are not its purpose. In love, all good things are realized. That is purpose enough.

Deep community, then, is communion before any effort to exploit the possibilities of life. Deep community should not be attempted casually. It is best when founded in a covenant, an agreement among members to open the doors of their hearts, to relate in common love and trust. Deep community is a radical departure from the thrust of ordinary community as organized relationships. It is best lived when informed by the enchantment of its members.

## Foreign Relations

Deep community embraces life in love. This includes, of course, other communities. Interaction with other communities is important for three reasons: 1) To prevent self-enclosure and social rigidity. 2) To promote personal, collective, and cultural evolution. 3) To prevent the loss of cultural integrity. The surest way to stop evolution is to prevent interaction and inclusion.

An enchanted community would be historically unique. Its existence could threaten other communities and be threatened by them. Even still, as the evolutionary imperative manifested in political and economic affairs, it would be hard to resist its literal manifestation.

## Community as Mentor

Deep community is the natural expression of enchantment when personal evolution is complete. Still, it is natural for any community to mentor its citizens. Communion, the social form of love, is a deeply inclusive transformative relationship. There is no teacher-student relationship. Individuals related to each other through their mentor are not in communion. They express organized activity. While this has been the historical preference as a teaching model in all spiritual traditions, it is now obstructive. Ordinary life is mentor to us all. We are daily instructed in the demands of evolution by the details and circumstances of our life. Every moment is now a potential evolutionary moment. Thus, an enchanted community is its own mentor. Individuals serving others as teacher and authority are not necessary. The most highly evolved members in any deep community always serve as leaders, but their presence is helpful, not essential, to the evolution of members. Deep community is a communion of colleagues and companions.

Since love is the model of relationship among community members, leadership roles are functional, not authoritative. In communion, democracy is transformed into consensus. Group awareness (independently achieved) is more important than group decisions since common awareness prompts common action. Consensus is spontaneous, unforced. Leadership is service, not authorized coercion. *Individuality* decreases. Creativity increases.

## Original Faith

We all live in love and faith because we live in a world we cannot avoid. Yet that is precisely our dilemma. We all know our lives are not entirely our own because we cannot prevent our connection to life. Life is always bothering us. We cannot fully control our life, and so we struggle. Life is an intrusion into experience.

### Faith Is All Around

Everyone has faith. But what is the *object* of your faith? Most of us trust what we can control, which of course is not really faith. It is trust of past experience. Such faith has an implicit escape clause: we will trust only after control is certain and only until it is no longer certain. Life is no more than a nonbinding contract. Such is the course of many relationships, if not most. But faith is unavoidable in all moments and circumstances because we cannot live even a millisecond without it: we must presume that the ordinary things in our life will not betray or destroy us.

Ultimately, and more than anything else, we trust our mind and, by extension, our knowledge. Knowledge is power. With power, we are no longer victims. Thus, knowledge is a hedge against faith, just in case our trust is violated. Knowledge is armament against ubiquitous and unknown terrors in an alien world of chaos and struggle. To the extent we know reality, we trust it. But, of course, we must trust our knowledge. So there is no escaping faith.

If you pursue separation and distrust far enough, you become psychotic, for you are trying to be literally nonexistent. Your reality becomes so unique and internal that you are either a threat, or useless, to yourself and others. To live an ordinary life then, faith must be present and active.

## Life Without Faith

We do not fear faith so much as we fear the need for it. We sense the gulf between self and the rest of the world. To function in the world we must trust. To function in the world demands we reach out. Touch it. Allow it to touch us. But the gulf is filled with unknown terrors and possible dangers. We are afraid of life and the unknown it contains. So, we trust, but hesitantly, suspiciously. We are conflicted in the most basic way. We are filled with anxiety and turmoil.

Knowledge becomes our way to make contact with reality while maintaining our distance and separateness. It is a hard lesson to realize that knowledge is insufficient for life without inner conflict. It is difficult to leave knowledge and embrace faith.

Our effort to manipulate the conditions of life and people, our pursuit of power, and related tendencies only demonstrate a fear of life. We structure our lives as defenses against change, the unknown. We try desperately to reduce or even eliminate the demands of ordinary life. Within this defensive structure, we can relax in its comforting protection. We trust our creation will not falter, crumble, or betray us. Yet our efforts can never avail us of the protection we seek. They fail, and fail repeatedly. We cannot relax or trust. We cannot protect ourselves against life.

So we search for safety and security, motivated by our chronic and pervasive sense of insecurity. Yet our search is doomed by what motivates it. How can we feel secure when insecurity is our most basic sense of reality? We live in a dilemma we cannot resolve. Our fear undermines our trust. Why do we emphasize reliability and responsibility if not because we want assurances our trust is not misplaced? We do not trust, but we must. The result is that our faith is surrounded by our fear. Fear is our protection against betrayal. Our need for ownership is part of a larger need to feel protected against possible betrayal and change (which is a kind of betrayal after all).

## We Must Trust What We Cannot Control

We cannot control everything. Regardless how deep our power or wisdom, we are never in unilateral personal control of our experience. It is true that our experience of life reflects the form of our faith and intentions, but it is also true that we are not alone in the world. Moreover, we must accept that even our own evolution is by nature beyond our control. It is not our intelligence or sensibilities, after all, that control the evolutionary process, but our interaction with life as a whole. So, at some point, we must accept our limitations. If we cannot accept that some things are beyond our control, we go mad trying to get control or explain why we can't.

It is our inability to control that motivates us to defend ourselves against life. Yet, we cannot really defend ourselves against life and still have a life. So we must paradoxically trust that which we presume could destroy us. And that is the real crux of our conflict with life. The conflict is with our presumption about life, not with life itself. So, again, we must surrender to life. Of course, we must not presume we are life's victims. We must not stop short of faith and fall into nihilism. We must live our lives fully, without struggle, not merely give up and call it fate.

## Confession

The hardest thing to do as you begin evolutionary learning is to *confess* you are utterly unworthy, powerless, without resources or recommendation, corrupted—well, you get the idea. This may seem silly or a complete affront. Either way, it is, for those very reasons, important to make such a confession. Why? It is necessary to begin with a clean slate. It is important to zero out the ego, to release anything the ego can attach itself to as a way to save face, survive, and ultimately to triumph in the battle to control your life and experiences.

This act of humility is an essential starting point if evolution is not to be compensation for personal deficiencies, or just another in your long list of personal triumphs. The confession must be energetically real, honest, true of you. You are not convincing anybody of anything. It is not a formality, but a sincere act of one who truly understands that what they seek is literally beyond the mind. Until you realize you cannot get there from here, that you cannot bootstrap yourself into enchantment, every thought and effort to evolve is doomed to fail.

This is difficult for many, impossible for some. It is anathema for those proud of their skills or achievements. It is impossible if you want a way to feel good about yourself, a way to improve your life experience. It is for those ready to quit posturing, to stop trying to be whoever you think you ought to be, and relent from the effort to live.

The second hardest thing to do is to confess you are simply and literally perfect, complete, and infinite. Between these confessions are all spiritual paths, all human endeavor and insight. But evolution is not moving from the first confession to the second. It is embracing both insights simultaneously, holding them, integrating them, using the creative tension of their interaction to enchant the world. Every enchanted being travels the full distance between those two insights. Some of us fight to gain self-respect or the respect of others, some fight to ward off arrogance. In love, you are always living both insights. You are always weak and blind, powerful and brilliant. Faith confesses both emptiness and fullness. In truth, all things are true of you.

We are both more than we dare hope and less than we dare imagine. It is important not to hope or imagine because such actions occur too late in the moment to do any good. A confession must be an honest embrace of life's fullness, prior to the moment where you arrive. Evolution occurs prior to the moment of personal awareness. It occurs when you are not home to be pleased or dismayed about what occurs. And this is not a single act, but an ongoing process.

## The End Is the Beginning

The original self is constantly embracing life without conditions or boundaries. Why leave that to the end of your path? Why not begin your evolutionary journey where you want to end up? Why not simplify matters and just practice being where you want to be rather than struggling to get there? Why not skip the unnecessary insights? The distance between you and enchantment is the idea that there is a distance. This is another way of saying there is no way to prepare for enchantment. There is always and only being and beginning in each moment. That is the practice.

If you seek some special form of life, some special condition or circumstance where your life experience will be just so, then you seek sanctuary, not evolution—quite a different matter. From the first then, you must accept your life as it is in this moment, as the full, complete, perfect expression of life's goodness. Obviously, that is easier said than done. We must always confront our fears while we try yet again to trust. Yet, only by embracing what you do not already understand can you come to understand. What you must understand, of course, cannot be said in words. It is not an idea, but an energetic and perceptual shift. You cannot understand what you avoid.

## The Way of Nonavoidance

Love is a life of nonavoidance. When you no longer avoid life, your efforts to exploit its resources collapse completely. You no longer try to control your experience of life. You no longer separate yourself from life in order to manage yourself. You no longer try to guide yourself through the treacherous waters of life. Rather, you embrace life fully. You accept life as true and not false; as reality, not illusion; as perfect, not imperfect. Your natural inclination then is to stop wondering if your life is perfect and start understanding how your life is perfect. You skip your doubts. You assume your life is founded within the presence of love. Your life is what you formerly sought. Now you must understand love rather than keep wondering where it is. Your questions and concerns no longer imply avoidance. Now your interest is only to understand what life is like and how it works when it is perfect in love.

Ask questions like "how could that be true?" Or, "if that is true, then what else must be true?" Seek to understand rather than be convinced. Accept your life as the *vehicle* of evolution, not its result. You will not know what you are doing, but your embrace is enough. Understanding comes later. In effect, you hold yourself accountable to live in accord with your intent. This involves observation and dismay (when there is no congruence), and joy (when there is).

By embracing your life fully, by not pulling back, distrusting, trying to manage your experience, you understand (achieve congruence) and accept your life. You understand and accept others rather than cynically reject their obvious stupidity. Compassion for yourself and others slowly emerges. You are less eager or able to make snap judgments. You allow the truth of life, the original intent of love, to emerge. You let life show you its wisdom, rather than decry its absence. Life is now good. It makes sense. You feel closer to the enchantment of life on earth.

In faith, you are in direct and continual interaction with what traditional paths approach only tentatively if at all: ordinary life. Love obliterates all paths. There is nowhere to go. Where can any path take you? There is always only life, and you are already there. *That* is where you make your life work, not in some middle-class vision of life that exists in some other time and place.

## From Here to Enchantment

In love, your way of life is the full embrace of ordinary life. How else can we live? What other way of life is possible? In love, your spiritual path collapses and disappears. You directly embrace the inherent intelligence and power of life within the ordinary. This simplicity and directness has a most profound result. Since your path is not a way to make life more spiritual and less ordinary, there is nowhere to go after realization. Life continues in ordinary circumstances. You do not escape from ordinary life into the waiting arms of an ashram with staff and students. Without the mitigation of a tradition, the moment after realization is profoundly revealing. In the moment of realization you cease to exist. The self-concerns that filled your awareness before that moment vanish. As you fall back into ordinary life after realization, you are profoundly and centrally aware of what was previously only on the periphery of your awareness: others.

Without *you* at the center of awareness, life floods in. You must make a choice you would otherwise have been spared. Life has not changed, but your relationship to it has. With the awareness and insight of realization available to you, you experience your life less as the context of realization and more as the object of realization. You notice the need for global enchantment.

So, you have stepped in it again! Rather than a cozy life of peace and wisdom, peace and wisdom become tools to engage life on a much bigger scale. Life has inconveniently knocked on your door once again. You are aware that the fullness of life has not arrived yet. Evolution has gone from being internal and personal to being external, impersonal, interpersonal. You have now gone global!

Life is pushing on you. You must choose how to push back, or whether. But the choice has already been made, really. Your life is about the embrace of life. If there is more life to embrace, how could or why would you stop? The skills of realization are the tools of evolution. On the other side of realization, you directly experience the limits, the pain and suffering, of others as your own. You were never living merely your own personal life, but now that truth is driven home quite forcefully. Now you must push back at life. You must immediately move beyond enjoying realization to using it for the sake of the collective original self that has emerged, a self that includes not only other people but the infinity of life. Your life is about the enchantment of life on earth.

## The Secret Process

The life of love begins where traditional spiritual paths end. You do not learn how it all is and then go live your life. You go live your life and then learn how it all is a manifestation of love. Love is the natural spiritual path embedded in ordinary life. Any formal path is an imposition on this most natural way of life. Love is the secret that makes all spiritual paths possible and effective. It is the key to the enchantment of life on earth. It is your love and trust in whatever you are doing or being at the moment that opens the door to learning, change, healing, evolution. We empower whatever we trust. It is not what we trust that empowers us. So, whatever you reject as an illusion and an obstacle to your life, you must ultimately accept as that which you seek. You end up where you begin, and you end up embracing what you thought you had to leave. In this way you gain power for the enchantment of life on earth. There is no way to learn love. There is only the relentless practice of what you think is love, and a deepening suspicion that what you practice is not love. We all stumble our way into enchantment.

## Trust

You learn to trust by not doing anything else. That is the long and the short of it. You are *present* when you are not somewhere else. You learn who you are by not trying to be someone. You trust others when you stop expecting them to be different. Trust neither confirms nor denies. It just allows. Trust is allowing peace between your self and reality. Trust is not trying to be separate from reality. Trust, faith, love are our default settings at birth. Everything else we learn later and, as you can see, it only complicates the simplicity and joy of our original self.

What you think you do when you trust is give up. What you really do is both give in and give up. You relent. You let reality alone. You let yourself alone. In a single act of trust, you free both yourself and the world you live in. We view trust as defeat in the battle of life—an admission of failure, self-betrayal. But that depends on where you stand. To the thinking self, trusting the original self is a betrayal. To your original self, trusting the thinking self is confidence. Confidence or betrayal? It depends on where you stand.

To trust is to forsake your preference for the thinking self (ego, mind, illusions, attachments, desires). Trust converts your identity from part to whole. To trust is to stop being less than you really are. Trust is not what you do before enchantment. It is the activity of enchantment itself.

## Being Trust

As an original human being, an enchanter of life, your trust enlivens the world, connecting you directly to life. Through you, healing life energy enters a wounded world that feels lost and abandoned. Your life projects nothing personal into the world because there is nothing to project. There is only life. You have already forsaken the illusion of a self that is separate from life, and so you project nothing of a separate self into life. You are empty. You are invisible.

As you descend into ordinary life, you do not have the option of being impersonal. You must be present as something rather than nothing. Love is the root of personal genius and the power to enchant life on earth. You begin by literally creating a self. But the self you create is not an act of personal whimsy. Your life becomes a playful, creative, healing, mythic interaction. Who and how you are in the world becomes a creative response to how best to enchant life on earth.

## The Enchanter: An Original Human Being

Enchantment, however, is more than most people want. Your presence opens an intuitive door others try to keep shut. You reveal more about them than they want to know. To deal with you they must deal with themselves. Often, then, you are not viewed as a gift of life and light, but as a destroyer on a personal quest for power. You demand more life, more responsibility, a fuller embrace of life than they find comfortable. You confront their limits. Their reflexive action is to avoid or attack. An enchanter of life reveals the line between life and death, and we must choose.

As an original human being, you live as an enchanter of life. Your life is both ordinary and miraculous. Nothing is unaffected by your presence. You live in the moment ahead of people's experience. You see what they do not yet see and do not want to see. You catch them off guard.

It seems to others that you are fully in control, in power. But from your perspective, you see only a continuing engagement of life just prior to the moment of awareness, that moment where there is literally nothing. Thus, you feel vulnerable, not empowered! What to others is genius, to you is only revelation. What to others seems planned, to you is spontaneous. What to others seems a disregard of their concerns, to you is trust before their concerns.

## Faith Is Not Belief

Faith is trust, acceptance. Deep faith is trust without boundaries or conditions. What churches or spiritual groups call faith is often closer to belief than trust. Faith is not belief. It is prior to belief, prior to what you know, hope, or imagine. To muster such a profound level of trust is to understand life can be trusted. This understanding is faith.

Each day brings something unexpected. Each day we confront our ignorance. We spend our life trying to contain our ignorance, yet in the end it remains. All of our activities are efforts to restructure reality so it can be known before we act. We struggle to create comfort, a hedge against chronic insecurity, a defense against the possibility of failure or death. But really, in our hearts, we know the whole thing is an artifact of our fearful creativity, a sham, a house of cards. Each day we must trust because if we don't, we cannot really live.

Faith is mind at the speed of light, universally present and still.

Faith is not living without proof; it is living before proof.

Faith is not understanding life; it is being life.

Faith is lived, not possessed.

There is no freedom without faith.

There is no salvation in faith. It is not a refuge from life.

Faith does not justify irresponsibility, nor excuse stupidity.

When faith is not constantly affirmed, it is explicitly denied.

Faith is nonavoidance of life.

## Blind Faith, Deep Faith

Faith increases awareness. Blind faith increases ignorance. There is no understanding in blind faith. It is blind. There are no reasons for such faith. It is bigoted, unreasoned, more emotion than thought, and definitely not intuitive. It is an effort to short-circuit thought and outwit the mind. It is a form of irrationality. It is useful ignorance. Such faith may be a comfort and a consolation, but it does not show the way to life, to intelligence. Such faith almost always has an object of faith located outside the believer. This is unawareness masquerading as trust.

Deep faith, however, is fully aware. It believes everything, hides from nothing. It embraces everything. It fears nothing. It trusts everything because it trusts before it can know. It trusts so it can know. Deep faith is the open attention and awareness that precedes all understanding and knowing. Thus, deep faith is not an alternative to knowing. It is the means of knowing.

Blind faith is blind belief. It destroys your mind, your reasoning, your awareness. If you force the mind to believe, you limit awareness. Rather than a tool of life, you have a monument to your fears. To believe anything to the exclusion of anything else is to end intelligence. To believe everything is to accept everything as true. Your task then is to understand what you believe. All that you remember comes from an encounter with life. All that you know, you extrapolate from such encounters. Would it not be better to encounter life than to remember it? Be less concerned with knowing than with seeing. When life is perceptual rather than conceptual, there is love.

## First Choices

When you love, you embrace the details of your inner life *and* your outer life, intuition *and* logic, your fears *and* your courage. All things as expressions of a common voice, a common source. All things are only one thing, parts of a single whole. Thus, conventional choices are pretty much impossible. Conventional life is unintegrated. It expresses conflicts within and between our inner and outer lives. We are aware of only some aspects of our reality and we trust only parts of that. This is the context of our choices. Our decisions result from pitting pros against cons, valuing some information over others. Decisions reflect distinctions rooted in conflict.

In love, all of life is one source of information and intelligence. Love democratizes reality, giving everything equal influence. In love, decision-making is not majority rule but unanimous rule. There is no inner voting, only inner being. There are no decisions or choices. One thing is not separate from another, so you cannot choose one thing over another. There is only awareness and a continuous choiceless choice. As the elements of your inner life work out their differences, inner congruence emerges. At last the entire energy field is unified (for the moment). It speaks with a single voice. You act with uncommon assurance and power. Nothing is complicated here, no moving parts. It is all radically simple. You are simple, uncomplicated.

Now that life is simple, you dance with life. You live in the world your inner and outer lives conspire to create. You do what is effortless, what you already have power and motivation to do. You follow the play of your inner and outer muses. Of course, this is how it goes when it all goes well. And we each find our own special way to screw things up. However it goes, the process will phase between apparent and real indecision (waiting for consensus), and spontaneity (acting on consensus). Decisions result from micro-epiphanies, small holistic shifts in the consensus of voices you call your self. The process of evolution begins imperceptibly.

I never recommend love as a place to begin a spiritual practice. Love should be your last resort, not your first. Until you exhaust your interest in all other options, you will always find a reason to put off evolution. Remember, conversion to love demands you unequivocally renounce and forsake all strategies but love. Until you commit to that most forcefully, your life will remain unconvinced of your purpose. It will not bend to wishful thinking.

## Personal Crisis and Decisions

In love, choices reflect passion, not logic. Decisions and actions are identical. Actions result from increased energy and create an evolutionary shift. We experience this increased energy as confusion, crisis. Thus: energy builds, you enact the energy, the crisis resolves. Evolution.

At other times, energy builds and there seems no choice to make, no action to take. Often, this precedes a coming shift in an energy pattern that informs your life profoundly. You fail to notice solutions because you have a blind spot. The pattern that is changing is something you assume is real and legitimate. You take it for granted. It does not occur to you at first that this can be a problem. Often, the problem is the solution. The choice you must make is a choice you know of but do not want to make. You think you have other choices. Hence, solutions elude you, at first.

Pressure mounts. Waiting and trusting that the issue will resolve itself in love brings no relief and no prospect of relief. You doubt. You pay closer attention. You feel stuck. You try technical solutions. They fail. You are distracted from other aspects of your life. As the energy continues to build, your choices become clearer, simpler. You find yourself resisting choices because they all seem bad. You know what you must do, but you don't want to do it. You hold out for other options. None appear. Finally, you are forced to act or go mad or watch your life tank. You act. The crisis resolves, sometimes fully, sometimes not. This may be part of a larger pattern that has not yet fully healed. Almost always, your best action is the one you wanted least to take, the one you most resisted. Notice there has been no reference to logic or thought. This is not about thinking your way out of a problem. You seek evolution, not mere change. Finally, notice this is a messy process. Evolution is not the end of a syllogism. It is learning. Learning is messy.

## Global Crisis and Decisions

This messy process is the same for individuals and groups. Global evolution is beyond the scope of this book, but the principles are the same. The difference is that the stakes are higher. There is more energy, organized in more complex ways.

Group energy is unstable because it is individualized. With certain precautions, we use the individual intelligence of a leader to organize groups. Every group has its alpha decision-maker. Individual intelligence is extrapolated into group settings. Group intelligence requires evolved individuals and an extension of that evolution into a group setting, creating deep community.

## The New Age

Many people talk of the end of an age. Most of us have a sense this is coming. It defies logic, but then so does adolescence. An age ends when an evolutionary shift is required for humanity to move forward. Life must be reorganized in new, higher, more complex forms if it is to proceed.

An evolutionary shift is systemwide. You can often tell an evolutionary crisis is at hand because there is a history of technical solutions that fail or work only marginally. Problems repeat. Old problems reappear in new forms. There are many ways the drama of failed technical solutions can play itself out, but ultimately resolution comes as system failure or revolution.

But revolution is just another technical fix that does no more than replace actors in a drama of stunted evolution. Real group evolution takes time and begins with a new energetic pattern at the individual level. Otherwise, people change or the group fails (does not survive) or downshifts into a less evolved pattern that matches the pattern of the individuals in the group.

## Democratizing Evolution

We are on the brink of a global evolutionary shift. We are certainly in need of one. We can all recount by rote the litany of crises in every area of human existence. The common denominator in them all is the nature of the individual human being. If we could change people, problems would solve themselves. Individuals. That is the problem and the solution. The problem is the solution!

The problems we face defy logic and technical solution. This is an energetic drama, not a logical one. Personal myths are the root of global myths.

Everything must change for anything to change. The choices we face during evolutionary shifts are all unfortunate. They require systemwide changes personally and globally. We are not going to dance merrily into our future because we say the right mantra, attend the right seminar, have the right insights, contact the right guides, hug a tree, get a personal coach, drum, or go to sweat lodges. That is not how we evolve.

People, organizations, countries, entire worlds all die for one reason: they cannot evolve. An evolutionary shift on a global scale is possible. It is always possible. Whether we move forward or not depends on whether we can stand naked before our machinations and surrender them all into the transforming fire of love. If we open up to evolutionary learning, to changes in primal patterns and forces we thought or hoped were dormant, the future will be more than we can dream. But human life must restructure itself. It must evolve to a higher level of intelligence.

## Pushing Evolution

On the other side of personal evolution is global evolution. What do we do with that? We face an issue of personal integrity and power. We are outnumbered and alone in the world. We can fit in and live a lie, or push back, make the world safe for love. Either way we are in for a struggle. If we fit in, we lose the integrity of our purpose. If we push back, we are a thorn in the side of the world. The world pushes against challenges to its integrity. And so the struggle continues.

Personal power and intelligence must shift into still higher forms. Global evolution begins at home. The lessons of love now serve you well. You must confront problems not of your making. You must learn to engage life without struggle outwardly, as you did inwardly. Pushing evolution does not mean struggle, but creativity. Evolution is a creative process. The evolution you now seek is no longer merely personal. It is interpersonal, global. We must find creative ways to make the shifts for global evolution. We are in a mythic struggle, not a literal one.

Your creative solutions, whatever they are, will not be the means for global evolution. The world will not flock to your doorstep eager to see what you have created. Rather, your solutions will be all that survive the old energetic patterns. You do not create the future by struggling with the present. You just create the future. Let the present old patterns die a natural death.

## The Mythic Battle

Pushing evolution is not a power struggle. There is nothing personal here. Your conversion to love was an act of personal global magic that altered reality from a merely personal drama into a mythic evolutionary play. We are unaccustomed to thinking in these terms.

Love brings you immediately into the world of mythic powers and forces. Conversion shifts your perspective of reality from personal to mythic. You must remind yourself that from this mythic perspective, the players in your life—the events and people that help or resist you—no longer act out of merely personal concerns. From the perspective of love, they express mythic powers and archetypes. To view them any other way is to miss the point and power of the play.

You notice others regard you in a personal way, as one whose life is driven by personal issues. The disorganization in your life, for instance, is viewed not as a prelude to evolution but as a personal failure to focus. If you interpret the behavior of others as personality driven, you miss their mythic import in your life.

On the upside of evolution (ascending path), your focus is internal and passive. On the downside (descending path), your focus is external and active. You are accustomed to allowing change to occur internally. Now change occurs externally. Trust is not enough. Now you must act, too. You must push evolution into the world. You are focused, not fixed; persistent, not insistent; creative, not confrontational. But people do not want what you offer. It demands too much. They are unconvinced dramatic change is needed. Your solutions will not improve their life in the short run, which is what they want. So, not everything will go as you want. You are not in control. You have self-mastery, not world mastery. Your inner life is simple and easy, but your outer life is a jumble of other people's energies. You find the world resisting you on occasion. You wait, or try something more creative. You persist. You do not give up.

On the other side of personal evolution is a test of your ability to survive in a world that needs you but does not want you. Be creative. Meet the challenge.

# Evolution: Death and Rebirth

Death is the mythic archetype of evolution because it guards all that is new. Death is not the end of life, only the end of the old pattern of life. We all know that, but we do not believe it. Our instinct for survival is largely a fear of death, not hope for new life. Fear of death may be key to survival in this life, but it is the core obstacle to evolution. Only when death is internalized can evolution occur. Interestingly, the internalization of death is the very definition of eternal life. Fear of death, then, is ultimately a fear of eternal life. The way to eternal life is through the death of our mortality. And where there is death without the end of life, there is evolution.

Fear of death expresses as a fear of relaxing, an inability to trust. We sense we are on the brink of death—nonexistence—as we approach unself-consciousness. The loss of our sense of separateness is the loss of our sense of being alive. To be alive is to resist the loss of separateness. It motivates all our activities prior to evolution. It enforces our search for control and power. The only power greater than our fear of death is trust. Even those who fear death trust their fear!

So, again, there is no way to live without trust. We are energetically connected to life and that connection is our trust, our faith, our love. Our unavoidable connection to life is a dilemma for anyone fearing death (the loss of separateness). Fear (of death) prompts continuous efforts to avoid life. We constantly resist, avoid, fear, ignore life in hopes that we can gain control over our separateness. We seek always to end our link to life, over which we have no control.

Anxiety, tension, paranoia, phobia—all express a fear of death that is really a fear of life and change. Fear is the archetypal pattern that most strongly influences our lives, our choices and actions. Fear is both the cause and the effect of alienation and separation. All the strategies and methods, defenses and motives known to mankind and history express our fear-based play of life. In the midst of our struggle with life over the power to control our separateness comes meek love.

For each of us there comes a time when we play out the game of life and find nowhere else to go. We are face to face with death. For each of us there is a central theme in our life, a covert purpose or agenda being served that we experience and illustrate on the canvas of our lives. It is this secret purpose that eventually runs out of gas, completes its journey or bankrupts our resources. Death comes. We are all stalked by death, by our personal network of illusions and limits, any or all of which could kill us, end our ability to survive. But death is not the end. We can survive death, but to do it we must evolve.

In some moment, you sense the need for change. You sense the frustration of your life quest. Nothing works. Your goal is unachieved. You cannot build the world you seek. It is then you notice death. You review your life, notice the increasing frequency of defeat, of emotional negativity and depression. You see the circumstances and conditions of your frustration, over and over. You are increasingly unable to cope. You search frantically, desperately for solutions. You are the victim of a personal yet anonymous tragedy. You are a casualty of war. You are losing the battle and you do not know why, or how. You feel pressure and unrelenting tension. You feel overcome by responsibilities. You want to shirk them, yet you feel you cannot or must not. Nightmares increase. Sleep also increases. Diversions increase. The desire to escape increases. Life is now a prolonged anguish and agony. You flail about, desperate for help. None comes. Your calls go unheard. No one understands you. All possible solutions are impossible. You look for alternatives but there are none. You withdraw. You are defensive and unhappy. You are without hope or recommendation. Your life is a living hell. You welcome death.

Now you must choose. Embrace death and evolve. Withdraw and die. Your only choice then is how to die. If you attempt a life of love before this crisis, you will turn back at worst. At best you will find another way to avoid death a bit longer. It is only when you face death that you can choose life, and begin anew in love. People who attempt love prior to this crisis make earnest efforts to do the right thing, but they become frustrated and often retort they tried love and it did not work. They are insincere. They want convenience, consolation, comfort—not love. It may seem cruel, but such people have not suffered enough. They have not exhausted their energetic options. They think they have choices. They are bargain hunting in the spiritual supermarket. They have not come to their real crisis of love and faith. Conversion is not yet possible.

People object to the idea of crisis and suffering as necessary prerequisites to love. I have no argument. It would be nice if life were not that way, but the logic of life is its energy. The choice to convert your life to love is largely forced on you by an increase in energy (tension) that cannot be diluted or avoided. It forces you to evolve or die.

Evolution is a shift in all your energetic patterns, not just some. Therefore, you can hold back nothing from life if you are to internalize your confrontation with death. To hold back nothing is to relinquish your separateness. To relinquish separateness is love. Love challenges your identity and existence. It brings the momentum of your old life to an end. This crisis is not an insight. It is a death. It is an energy shift in what is possible and necessary. When love is only a good idea, evolution will not result, only death.

Rebirth is a return to the energetic pattern of your original self. What dies is the separateness of the thinking self. Rebirth lets us to return to our original pattern of love and from that place of simplicity, power, freedom, trust, and community we move back into life. The result is evolution.

## Love Is Your Guide and Teacher

A true crisis of faith (death) signals evolution. The habits of your nervous system are breaking down. Now you can learn energetically. The original self, always receptive to life's energies, has a permanent learning relationship with life. Your body receives the instruction, information, guidance, and wisdom of life more easily, now that old habits are collapsing. The body learns from literally everything. All you ever need is always right before you.

Our optimal condition is always our original condition. Eventually, the mind swoons in the embrace of the body. The two become one. Follow your inclinations. Life and your body are conspiring to bring you fully to love. Any and every sort of teacher can help you, but no one can love for you. This is your journey. Only you can make it.

### Enquiry: Building Awareness

Attend to what goes on in your life. Ask, is this love? You will notice serendipities, unexpected opportunities. Some things will be easier than others. Trust your instincts. Embrace your life in each moment, but do not focus on any one thing. Be fully attentive to life in all dimensions. Trust your inner and your outer life. Do not fear confusion.

You have not learned something because you can describe what you think is different. Evolutionary learning is energetic, nonconceptual. Trust that you are learning even when you cannot sense anything at all. Relate to life as your personal guide. Trust it as real and good. Sometimes we want a peek into the future. We want to get ahead of the curve, anticipate the inevitable, get a sense of control. Relax and trust. When you see the future, you also see that until the future arrives you must play out the drama of your role (the archetypal energies in your life). Even when you know what is ahead, how you get there is still a mystery and more important than where you arrive. Thus, you are always drawn into the present moment. Accept it and learn from its energy.

Guidance is the power of personal intent. Intentions are as small as butterflies, as big as the arc of creation throughout eternity. As you practice love (intent, faith, attention, action) you gain an intuitive sense of what is appropriate in the moment, what is workable or not. You see relationships everywhere. This is the beginning of intelligence. You search for the right thing to do in the moment, but there is no right or wrong doing. There is only a right or wrong being. Your choices and actions are not the result of deciding, but of discovering in the moment.

Look for the immediate, the obvious. Do not try to outwit life. Embrace it. Do what feels effortless, immediate. It is a simple formula. Accept all things as true. This is the rule of love.

# Original Meditation

And so, we arrive at the moment when we must practice surrendering to our body's intent to love in a pragmatic way. I do not recommend meditation as a practice. Life is your meditation. And, while I have consistently emphasized the need to relax, I do not recommend relaxation strategies either because, as we shall see, they all inhibit the possibility of evolution. That said, I do recommend Original Meditation. It is, in a way, an anti-meditation practice. It has no focus but to succumb to the original self, whose nature and activity is love. This allows the body's wisdom to influence you. The thinking self is not in control. It just relaxes into the body's habit of love. Nothing is forbidden. Everything is allowed. Nothing is avoided. Everything is embraced. No boundaries or barriers. You are surrendering to love in the body. Welcome to enchantment.

## Original Meditation as Love

The healing process that uncovers the wisdom and power of the original self is entirely energetic. Evolution occurs at levels too subtle for ordinary experience. Not only can evolution *not* be self-directed, then, but you need a means to induce the healing process that allows it to proceed of its own intelligence. The strategy I used (Original Meditation) induced enlightenment in under four thousand hours of formal practice (five months actual time, five years elapsed time). It is an energetic process that is inherently freeing and healing. Original Meditation could not be simpler. All forms of meditation actually complicate, and so hinder, this simple, powerful, strategy.

Original Meditation (OM) is the practice of love. It induces change *before* experience. Change cannot occur as quickly or intelligently any other way. OM is self-transcending. Because the practice is effective before self-control and awareness occurs, it soon becomes the context of attention. This allows all moments to be moments of deep change and love. The formal practice of OM leads to an informal habit of attention within intuitive awareness. Thus, the evolutionary process of love becomes automatic, generalized in your life, no longer requiring formal practice.

## Original Meditation as Learning

The practice of love optimizes personal and collective intelligence because it is an intentional effort to be open-minded. As you stop controlling your mind, it is free to be more intelligent. The result is that brain function improves due to improved attention and awareness.

Since everything is energy, and love opens you to all energetic activity, the mind and body learn in response to everything in your life. Everything serves your transformation. The ways you resist life (knowingly or not) are in continuous play with everything in your life. As you relax, you free the interaction between life and your inhibitory habits. Life always wins. Love succeeds.

OM is a strong antidote to any tendency to withdraw or stay safe within familiar boundaries. OM is an act of relentless courage. Learning in love is pragmatic, concrete, nonconceptual, and nontheoretical. OM does not filter or modify the impact of life. OM encourages an unconditional embrace of life in all moments so all things are noticed, appreciated, loved. OM is a way to learn. Understanding yourself comes only after you sincerely and deeply engage life in love, not before. Love is living your life before fear, so in every moment you are at play in an enchanted world.

## Relaxation: Being the Body

OM is more a relaxation strategy than a meditation practice. But relaxation strategies help the body relax by distracting the mind with something to do. As you use this prophylactic for your mind, the body relaxes since it is disconnected from the continual interference of the mind.

OM does not distract the mind to ease the body. It integrates the energetic habits of the mind and the body, transforming both. OM does this by *not* using a technical means to relax. Doing so enforces a disconnect between mind and body. Instead, OM relies on the body itself and your willingness to allow everything, avoid nothing. It relies on a relentless choice to trust the body.

## Freedom: No-Habits

Original Meditation is rooted in no-habits. No-habits means you do not cling to thoughts, images, feelings as you relax. Not all habits are bad, of course, but there is no sunset law for them. They persist even when their value is gone. Much of our life is lived by habit. It is easy to be unaware. It is essential then to release habits so we can respond intelligently to life rather than habitually. To cling to anything is to prefer one thing over another, leaving something unloved. Let things enter and leave your life and your awareness without effort, resistance, or suffering.

## Love: No Desires

Original Meditation is nondesiring. Love embraces all things, all possibilities. Desires limit awareness and effort. They imply fear of not getting what you want. None of this facilitates evolution. You cannot love what is not present in the moment. You cannot use, integrate, or learn from anything that is not present. To desire what is not present is to avoid what already is. Let love be your strategy on your evolutionary journey. Approach all things by being present in this moment of love.

## Being: No Doing

With OM, you quite literally do nothing! And that is the problem, if that can be a problem. Its utter simplicity often goes unnoticed beneath the torrent of mindful activity. We tend to be more complicated than the practice. Most people who think they are practicing Original Meditation are not because they are doing something, usually out of habit. If you are doing anything, you are doing too much. Doing interferes with being, embracing life by not avoiding it.

## Simplicity: No Complication

OM is deeply simple. It does nothing. That is its advantage. It imposes nothing on the current of consciousness. You allow everything. You are the meditation. You do nothing. You become everything. OM knows nothing needs be done. The body is already in love. Just don't interfere.

Here are three details about the practice of OM:

## 1. *Acceptance*: Nonavoidance

Embrace the moment, fully and deeply. Period. Life occurs in five realms at once. Accept the fullness of life, in this and all other moments. When you accept life fully, you accept its intelligence, its love, its power. You allow all the original qualities of life into *your* life. Life is the natural and archetypal spiritual path. We need no other.

The Inner Practice

OM is embracing life. It is complete, unselfconscious immersion in the roar of life. No effort is made to maintain your self/identity or awareness, to survive, or even to exist. Thus:

- Sit down. Close your eyes. Relax. Let go.
- Make no further effort to relax, to be aware, or to do anything at all.
- End the practice when it occurs to you to do so.

That is all. I told you it was simple. It may not seem like much, but it is the most powerful evolutionary strategy you can practice. Remember that whatever happens is all right. Regardless of what happens, let it happen. Do not worry. Move to the next moment. Let your mind, your self, *fall* into the stream of consciousness without effort to be aware of what is going on, without trying to remember or learn anything. Do not worry if you fall asleep.

This becomes a very *intense* practice as the stressful habits of your nervous system come into awareness. You may find it difficult to relax without avoiding something. You may find it difficult to sit still! That's O.K. Get up. Walk around. Breathe deep. Shout or scream. Do what you must to remain engaged with the energy of the moment rather than avoid it. Express the energy in whatever way seems appropriate. Vent. Give in to whatever is happening in the mind or body. Do not observe it. Do not restrain it. Give in to it. This may not seem very *relaxing* because you are not *avoiding* stress, as with other relaxation techniques. You are releasing the *habit* of stress. You are relaxing the self-imposed barrier between mind and body. Allow yourself to dream. Give up control. The body is already in love. Let things be. Everything is part of the process of returning to being fully human.

Surrender your concerns. Abandon your cares and worries. Forsake your motives and strategies. Allow yourself to be free, neither affirming nor avoiding anything. Destroy your limits by embracing whatever is present. You need do nothing to destroy your limits. Just do nothing to energize them. Limits vanish with lack of attention. Remember your choice to love. Relax. Let go. Trust the inherent and magical power of your body.

This formal inner practice facilitates healing. It is useful to set aside time to do this without distraction. This formality increases the simplicity and effectiveness of the practice, since it is not complicated by other activities. It also facilitates the outer practice of Original Meditation.

## THE OUTER PRACTICE

The outer practice of OM is the practice of love in action. Remember that OM alone is insufficient for evolution. The inner practice establishes and stabilizes the inner process of love. It is essential that this inner habit generalize outwardly. Choices and expectations here are critical. They set the limits of your transformation.

Do not assume that all you need do is meditate and live your life as before. The habit of formless attention must be practiced while you are active in ordinary life, not just in formal practice. Love must be the inner *context* of your life. This emphasis on outer and inner practice confronts the scope of your purpose. Will you embrace life fully, or only in an armchair?

## THE PRACTICE OF INSIGHTS

*The insight of oneness.* Let everything that is, be what it is, as it is, when it is. Nothing more. Nothing less. Should thoughts arise, let them. Should they not appear, or disappear, or fail to reappear, let them. Should thoughts, images, memories or anything else dwell in your awareness for long periods, let them. Keep doing nothing—accepting, allowing. Keep on keeping on. Do not enforce emptiness. Should you fall asleep, don't worry. When you awake, make no judgment.

*The insight of life.* The force of life is sufficient for evolution. There is literally nothing to do or achieve. Experiences, insights, and healings occur at the proper time in their proper form, with their proper results. Accept what is present at the moment, fully understanding that what the next moment will bring will be different. The future is not a continuation of the past so long as you are free in the present. Freedom is the outcome of love. Evolutionary change is a natural process. It does not need to be created or forced. Therefore, again and again and again, everything must be allowed, nothing prohibited. There is only life, in love.

*The insight of presence.* The conditions for personal and global evolution are already present, active, functioning. Allow life to function fully, without your help. Confer freedom on all things. Let all things exist by their natural inclination, including your self. Let yourself be affected by all that comes to you, from you, through and around you. Abide.

*The insight of perfection.* You are perfect but unaware. It is not necessary to root out what you think is unhelpful. OM is not an effort to fix anything because the body is already perfectly in love. OM lets your body be your guide.

*The insight of conversion.* Conversion occurs when you see you are your worst enemy. Your perception of and relationship to life must be shifted, relentlessly, in love. Affirm your choice to love. Let awareness in love organize your life until you are fully converted to love.

*The insight of only-real.* Everything is real. The idea that there is an illusion is an illusion. In love, all things are real, true, and present. If a problem appears, it is an improper view of reality. Accept all things for what they truly are energetically, not what you think they are.

*The insight of engagement.* Love brings you to life, not away from it. Even though your practice is quiet and solitary, the result is a capacity to embrace life more fully. OM is not a substitute for activity. Love is our original relationship to all activities.

## 2. Attention

The second aspect of OM is attention, awareness. Do not *try* to pay close attention or observe. Rather, let your mind go in whatever direction it inclines.

### THE OBSERVER STATE

Observation is natural for the thinking self. It need not be practiced or enforced, unless you seek experiences. Observation requires you to focus and maintain attention. This limits awareness and evolution. So, relinquish observation and all forms of focused attention. Relax attention until it moves ahead of observing. Do not inhibit, promote, direct, or control your attention.

### THE PRIMORDIAL ONE

Attention will phase between observing, dreaming, and unselfconsciousness in the Void as it moves among and integrates all energetic realms in the body. As attention moves from the physical to the intentional realm, self-awareness is gradually shed until the self disappears in a mystic union with life. Here the capacity to observe is utterly lost. The boundaries of the self collapse. Then, as you move into the energetic realm, you swoon and faint. Awareness is lost, overwhelmed momentarily. All things, inwardly and outwardly, blink out. You die. The world dies. There is no self and no other. There is nothing: the Void.

This mythic journey to the primordial emptiness and back repeats with increasing intensity and speed. Phasing is how the Void of the Primordial Spirit and the realm of ordinary experience merge. With time, awareness expands to incorporate and integrate all realms into one, at which point phasing stops. The Infinite Self stands motionless in all realms and simply Is.

You are now the most dangerous person in the universe. *You* are everywhere. Everywhere is always here. The thinking self and original self merge and evolve into the Infinite Self. The age and reign of the individual is complete, and completed. The possibilities of the Infinite Self emerge slowly and become the Enchanter's Game. What happens next is not predictable.

NOTICE

Phasing occurs spontaneously as attention moves among realms. Do not avoid observing by seeking the Void. Watch. Notice. This is how insight usually comes. You need do nothing, nor consider the process from a special perspective. Just observe, attend. The body will bring to mind whatever is appropriate or needed. Remember, learning is energetic, not conceptual. Evolution is not a self-directed process. Avoid anything. Attend. Accept all things without reaction.

## 3. Sincerity of Intent

It does not matter what you want to be true or think is true. It only matters what is true. That you want to be sincere in your practice of OM will not affect your actual sincerity. How can you tell if you are sincere? Notice. Apply the process of love-faith-attention-action. Notice if what you do comports with what you intend. Verify what you are doing. It is your dismay about insincere practice that facilitates congruence between intent, purpose, and action.

OM allows the body's intent to overwhelm, purify, and organize your inner entire life. But the simplicity and power of OM itself is overwhelmed if your personal choice does not match the body's choice to love. OM is merely relentless repetition if your choice to love is insincere. Your sincerity is gauged by the times you choose to embrace what appears rather than react.

Be accountable. Sincerity allows life to affect you without fear. Sincerity is simplicity. There are no motives. OM is an act of love and deep honesty. If there is insincerity, there is subterfuge. The purpose behind your insincerity will overwhelm any other desired choice. It will be satisfied. If you practice OM with doubt, you will get what you suspect. In OM, there is only you.

## Summary

There may be other details that would embellish this description, but I think these are the true essentials. Nothing else is required. It is a simple practice, but hard to do, since there is really nothing to do. So long as you are sincere in your choice to love, all things will occur as needed.

Caveat: People who do not experience profound changes in their inner and outer lives resulting from OM generally are not practicing OM. The evolutionary power of OM depends on the scope of your *choice*. Purpose sets the context and direction for your life and, by extension, Original Meditation. Nothing in your life is more powerful than the energetic habit that is your true purpose and choice in life. That large numbers of people practicing meditation are not enlightened already is due entirely to the absence of a proper choice to love and all that entails.

## Spiritual Teachers

I am not a fan of spiritual teachers (if you had not guessed). It is an archaic metaphor and role with political implications not suited to evolution. Teachers are agents of a teaching, something to make learning easier, more structured. But this leads to learning a teaching rather than love.

The teacher-learner relationship is inherently disempowering. It is not a relationship of mutuality or community. It enforces an authoritarian agenda that generates followers, but not good companions on the path of love. Finally, spiritual teachers focus on enlightenment rather than evolution. The possibility I call enchantment includes the possibility of psychic and supernatural powers that appear spontaneously. The powers of enchantment are interesting, but not the point. We are here to live and love. Perhaps that does not seem like much of an agenda for life. But why must life be so complicated? It need not be. So, what about spiritual teachers?

## Intent in the Teacher-Learner Relationship

Spiritual teachers say desire is a prerequisite for enlightenment. Whatever you call it, it speaks to the issue of choice and purpose. Both teacher and learner are helpless in the face of the true energetic choice of the learner. When is proper choice absent? Whenever enlightenment is absent!

Enlightenment and evolution result from personal intent, not technique. There is no technical fix for the lack of proper personal intent. Life is the manifestation of your intent. The teacher can do and should do nothing about a lack of proper intent for evolution. Only you can alter it. Any effort by a teacher creates illusion and dependence. Of course, it is impolitic to tell a student their lack of success is due to a lack of sincerity. It is more conducive to creating a spiritual empire if you provide people with lots of detailed, but ultimately irrelevant, teachings and things to say and do.

Personal intent is not a matter of *stating* a purpose. It is holding yourself accountable for *living* your purpose. There is no formulaic practice for this. It is a matter of acting and noticing. Are you doing what you intended or not? If you will not hold yourself to your purpose, what good will practice do? If your practice of OM is at odds with your purpose, practice will do no good. If OM is congruent with your purpose, you do not need it. Either way, practice is irrelevant.

This simple process is more complicated when you ask someone to help you because you must trust that person. You must give them some influence in your life. A traditional devotional teacher-student relationship results. But devotion is not love. It is addiction.

To be a loving relationship, it must be mutual. Teacher and learner must overcome any and all implications and limits associated with those terms and become lovers (don't go there!). They must be mutually available to each other, in love and respect, as peers. What prevents this from becoming merely personal is that both parties are devoted not to each other but to love itself, the evolutionary process. Here they are companions (free and self-responsible people) in love. They are not using each other for their own ends, but enjoying each other's company and help in love.

When you meet a spiritual teacher, you usually want to know the teacher's qualifications. If you think the teacher is qualified, your prospects for success improve because you trust them. It does not occur to you that your faith is more important than their qualifications! Anyone can teach. Few can learn.

Questions a teacher and learner should ask each other: Who are you? What do you want? Why do you not have it? What have you done? What have you learned? What do you want from me? What will you offer me? There are no right or wrong answers here, but the answers will have meaning to both of you. You will both know if your personal intentions are the same.

You heal from what you love. You learn from what you love. You become what you love. If your purpose is love, then no good thing in life can be denied to you. You can have no purpose other than love and expect evolution. But in love, you cannot avoid it.

## The Dilemma of Spiritual Teachers

Can one person help another person evolve? People are energetic systems. Help works best when you have a technical problem, not an evolutionary one. Most people do not want to risk the stability and identity they have for the sake of evolution. It is too difficult and unpredictable. Instead, people endlessly pursue technical solutions, hoping their problem really is technical. They dismiss systemwide change as too much work. They want to know what to do (a technical approach). They do not want to be told to relax, alter perception, and embrace the problem!

Most people are followers, not leaders. They want to focus on detail, not overview. Love is a strategy, not a practice. At every turn, the practice is to remember your purpose and let your intuitive sense of congruence guide behavior. The only way to make love work as a strategy is to have a high tolerance for ambiguity and a will to be relentless for an entire lifetime. How many people do you know like that? For people who fit that description, there are two ways to help others. 1) Help others be responsible for their evolution. 2) *You* be responsible for their evolution. The first way is love. The second way is the way of gurus and masters.

To accept spiritual teachers as the mechanism of change you must view evolution as a technical problem with a technical solution, which it is not. A technical approach has never worked. If you can evolve in such a technical relationship, you do not need it. The only basis for an evolutionary relationship is mutual love, not unilateral necessity.

The guru tradition is so common because the technical methods of the guru make spirituality manageable. The guru turns evolution into a problem that expertise and proprietary technology can solve. Since evolution is a spontaneous system reorganization, outside intervention from a guru or teacher can produce technical changes, but the system only changes. It does not evolve.

Evolution is a systemwide response to failure and possible death that cannot or will not be escaped. Evolution demands and results in a systemwide shift in awareness and identity, of both purpose and process. A guru can, through various means, push a student into crisis so the student will make an evolutionary shift. But the intervention cannot generate the shift. The guru can only generate the crisis. A guru with certain skills can unilaterally alter a person's energy, but the student must be able to maintain the new pattern, or it will fail. But even if both people do their part, evolution does not result. Evolution results from a spontaneous systemwide shift in an energetic pattern where the alternative to evolution is complete breakdown (death).

Evolution is systemic self-reorganization. Evolutionary intelligence evolves from within. Indeed, it is the natural and inevitable result of a relentless and singular insistence on love in the midst of the changing drama of life. Without a relentless and unchanging response to ordinary life, evolution cannot occur. Evolutionary intelligence cannot come from outside the individual (i.e., the guru). Ordinary change occurs in the physical and psychological realms. Evolutionary change occurs in all realms, but is exemplified by change in the mythic and intentional realms.

The only way an intervention can help evolution is if it occurs before the moment of awareness and action for either the guru or the disciple. If both people can function in the moments of intention and faith, then they can and will spontaneously affect each other, with evolutionary results for both. But if the disciple can function this way, the guru is useful and helpful, but unnecessary. Such a spontaneous intervention is called the grace of the guru, but its power depends on the disciple, not the guru.

Evolution threatens all structures and systems, especially those not evolved. A new energetic system creates an inherent tension in every interaction with old, less intelligent, systems. Among human beings, whose comfort zone exists entirely within the predictable and the uniform, this new arrival is destabilizing. The evolution of one encourages the evolution of all.

Following the teachings of a guru or tradition dumbs down the follower. Your focus moves from evolution to precision, intelligence to expertise. This generates followers and technicians, not intelligent beings capable of self-direction, self-governance, and cooperative creativity.

The student's adaptation to a guru is a focused, technical response to a crisis only the guru generates. But evolution occurs when there is a systemwide organic response to an entirely new and *inescapable* environment demanding a higher form of intelligence for survival. The entire system must evolve and reorganize. For a student to do this says more about the student than the teacher. Intelligence is not an intervention. It is an internal shift of relationships among all components in a system. Evolution is not an addition to a system, but a transformation of it.

Technical change results from focus. Evolutionary change results from the absence of focus. The traditional emphasis on the powers, skills, and insights of gurus is misguided if your purpose is evolution. Indeed, structure thwarts evolution (a mutational process by nature). The outcome of evolution is neither predictable nor controllable. It disdains all efforts to make it that way.

The natural impulse of spiritual teachers to help undermines evolution. Their efforts produce only technical change, not enlightenment. Thus, we do not need teachers. We need ordinary life.

In the third age of humankind,
The age of the myth and maturity,
We lived to dream.

# The Enchanter's Game
## (Epitome & Evolution)

## To Dream Is to Love

YOUR DREAM IS YOUR PURPOSE IN life. Make it a good one. Until you are dreaming life, you are not living it. To love summarizes all we can be. To dream summarizes all we can do.

All that you have read so far is true, yet it is all prologue. Love is the simplicity that all other things complicate. Love is the key to learning and healing in all realms, but it is not sufficient for enchantment. For that, something more is required, something easier.

Be honest. Does not love seem more like a duty than a gift? Is it not something you want, but feel helpless to offer? Is not love just another reason, another way, to struggle in life? Well, just as we are hardwired to love, we are hardwired to dream. The body is in a constant dreamlike communion with life. And unlike love, dreaming is something we find easy to do.

We are born to love. We are destined to dream. First, we succumb to the body's dream of love: enlightenment. Then, we must dream and create a life of love: enchantment. To dream life in love is our true vocation. When you choose to dream, evolution begins. Who cannot love their own dream? Even when we put aside our dream for the sake of practicality, who does not secretly cherish it above all else? It is easy to love when you are living your dream.

## Reality Is a Dream

We believe what we are taught, what we experience. We believe physical life is real. It exists independently of us. The first age of humankind, childhood, is about physical life and survival. The second age, adolescence, is about power—self-assertion, competition, domination—patterns of adolescence. So, like any adolescent, we create a world where we compete to survive. In that age, we learn life is not about physical survival and prosperity, hopefully. We learn about the power and will of the gods. We are taught morality: to live well (to prosper), we must live properly (in accord with the gods). This is the lesson of adolescence, of the second age.

The shocking revelation of the third age, however, is that the gods do not have a will of their own, except in a most primitive way. The gods do not make the rules. They carry out the rules. The gods fulfill the will of another, higher, organizing principle: the dream.

## Life Manifests Dreams

Life is a dream, imagination manifested. How? We influence our bodies directly. The body is in constant two-way communion with all realms. Our inner life unavoidably manifests in and as our outer life. The *will of the gods* refers to personal choices, individually and collectively lived. The *Supreme Being* who rules us all is our body's intent to love as lived in our dreams.

The hope of a better self, a better life, a better world, need not be merely a thought. Dreams manifest directly in the physical realm, via the body. The problem is that we do not believe it.

## The Dream of Love

A dream has no power without love. Love has no purpose without a dream. Love is the power that enchants our world, but its power is contained in our dreams. The Tree of Life itself is nourished by the love in our dreams. A dream seizes our imagination and our life. Through the power of love held in our dream, we heal and mature. Finally, we outwardly express the creative power of love in our dream. At last the two are one. The dream is real. Love enchants the world.

We think skills or efforts create our dream, but it is not so. Our dream creates our skills and motivates our efforts. We think love creates our dream, but our dream is love manifested. It is our dream that orchestrates the body's natural learning/healing process (the spiritual path) that empowers us inwardly. Surrender to the dream. Align your life with it. Become love. Then create and live your dream as your gift to the world. What is your dream? The dream that is yours alone will always glow with the radiance of love that only you recognize and only you can live.

It might seem intelligent and expeditious to live as others do—you would be wrong. We are each uniquely inspired by a dream. Our lives express our dream or our struggle to live it. Focus on your dream alone. Let your life emerge from that. The sacred theater of unrequited love, evolutionary intelligence, all spiritual paths and life itself, are tacitly orchestrated by our dreams.

Is evolution too high a price to pay for your dream? Evolution is how we connect to our dream in love. You have no dream? Can't find it? Don't know what it is? Begin with anything that truly inspires you. Your unique gift of love to the world is in that direction.

## Evolution Is Intelligence and Health

Enchantment involves evolution that is not confined to the mind or body. Evolution begins as inner learning and healing, the most notable markers of which are conversion, enlightenment, and realization. The energetic changes of inner transformation stem from a natural learning and healing process we rely on every day of our lives: love. There is nothing peculiar or special about evolutionary learning and healing except its results. Inner evolution begins spontaneously when you surrender your life to your dream via the body. Evolution is the journey you take when you dedicate your life to your dream of love.

We naturally and easily move toward our dream so long as we hold it, believe it is possible, and allow *ourselves* to change so the dream comes true. We resolve the creative tensions of dreaming through personal inner learning and healing.

## Dreaming Is Magic

The core process of reality is magic. Magic is not the exception; it is the rule of reality. Dreams become reality when you surrender your life to them. The magic of love heals your inner and outer lives until your dream comes true. Once your inner learning and healing has progressed sufficiently and is stable, the power of your dream moves outwardly into the world. What else can it do? The power of your dream now impacts others and the world generally as it impacted you personally: healing, learning, creativity, intelligence, community. The world evolves and is healed as a higher order of life-affirming intelligence appears in human form.

The problem with magic as a means to influence physical reality is that we seek power before our inner life has purified and adapted to our dream of love. We want our desires (often not a dream of love) to manifest despite our inner condition. But our inner life manifests directly in the world. Until we perfectly establish our dream inwardly, we can only sabotage it outwardly.

## Global Learning and Healing

Enlightenment and other evolutionary changes occur best and most easily when we are inspired rather than disciplined. We are inspired to learn and heal by our dreams. We are able to learn and heal by the love contained in our dreams. By following our dream, by committing our lives to the journey of manifesting our dream, we induce all the learning and healing needed to make our dream come true.

How can you evolve in a way that easily, naturally, and quickly results in enchantment, the capacity to manifest your dream? The answer is in a single word: love. Follow your heart and you will become all you need to be to manifest your dream of love.

## Personal Evolution as Planetary Change

Learning and healing denote the inner process of self-transformation, evolutionary change, enlightenment. What is curious is that the bigger the dream (the more inclusive it is) the more quickly and easily it appears, and the fuller and deeper is your transformation. When you have mastered the inner process of learning and healing, any dream can be manifested outwardly. It is this further *magical* possibility that eludes most spiritual practitioners. The inner learning and healing process transcends its point of origin (your inner life) to affect physical reality.

This occurs because the definition of who you are is changing, evolving, incorporating inside everything you think of as outside yourself. You become all-inclusive. What appears to others as an ability to directly affect outer reality is for you only the result of an internal shift. This is the realm of magic and miracles. By mastering evolutionary learning and healing, physical reality becomes internalized. In other words, the assumed boundary between your inner world and your outer world collapses. Objective reality responds to you as your own body. You and the world are directly connected through the body's intent to love.

## Our Evolution into Magical Beings

Magical powers are often viewed as the result of precise mastery of techniques that generate specific results. But your dream, firmly held, shapes reality—not any technique! Trust your dream. You are wired to experience dreams as reality. Relax into yours and it will come true.

Enlightenment (the way of inner evolution) and enchantment (the way of outer evolution) are the result of adapting to the demands and logic of your dream. As you learn what your dream means and implies, you must choose it. As you affirm your dream, you give your self and your life permission to become the dream.

## The First Four Realms

The traditional three-part metaphysical model of reality is body, mind, and spirit. Body is the physical realm. Mind is the personal and mental realm. Spirit is the mythic realm of angels and gods. Personal evolution followed this pattern: body/childhood, mind/adolescence, spirit/maturity.

The beginning of the second age generated insight about a fourth realm, the energetic realm of unpatterned energy and creative power. This is the realm of the Primordial Spirit—Roar. The energetic realm suffuses the other three. It is the core of manifest reality: energy before it appears as thought, reality, or dream. This fourth realm makes magic possible. It directly connects all realms to each other. In this realm everything ceases to exist, even the gods (the mythic creative archetypes that organize and create reality). It is only in the energetic realm of Roar that you are ultimately free of all the patterns and habits of life and reality. You cannot dream here. The energetic realm is the end of dreaming. In this realm, all things end.

## Land of the First Born: The Fifth Realm

The beginning of the third age generated a vision of a fifth realm: land of the first born. All things begin in this land of first choice, or dreams. This is the first level of creation, prior even to the gods. Dreams are more subtle than thought, more powerful than gods. The originating idea or blueprint of all possibilities is here. The power of life is in the fourth realm, but the magic of life begins in the fifth realm.

Enchanters of life, who live in all realms and whose dreams affect all realms, surrender their life to their dream. They surrender into Roar, where the pattern and habit of their being dissolves into the formlessness of the Primordial Spirit. They emerge reborn, in the land of the first born, where all things begin. Inwardly empty of any prior purpose, they dream a dream of love that fills their being and directly impacts the physical realm. Magic, then, is the nature of life when life is lived in all realms. Magic shifts the experience and nature of life from an ordeal, to a game: the enchanter's game.

## The Two Paths of Magic

The enchanter's game of dreaming reality integrates the two major spiritual strategies: mysticism and paganism. It begins with the mystic or ascending path to Roar: you confess your story, release the burden of ordinary life, let attention ascend and awareness expand to infinity. The result is purification and freedom.

Confession is an act of personal honesty and integrity, a complete self-revelation. More importantly, it is an act of complete self-acceptance. To live your dream, you must make your inner life available to it. This occurs only through self-revelation, or confession.

The second step to manifesting your dream is to live it—make your life available to your dream. This is the pagan or descending path of manifestation and power, bringing the power of Roar into the physical world. Here you dedicate your life to your dream. You agree to live inside your dream rather than keeping the dream inside of you. You surrender your life to your dream.

## Who Are You?

The truth will set you free, but you are free already and there is no truth! Truth is just another word for a dream, and you decide on the dream. The problem is that you are trapped inside the illusion that there is no dream, there is only reality about which you have no choice. You are trapped in the matrix of your mind that says reality is given to you rather than created by you.

There are entire spiritual paths dedicated to awakening from life's illusions. But awakening is not the end point of spirituality! It is just the beginning. Once you awaken, you still must choose to love, and the specific form your love takes in the world is your dream. You must live your dream or you will only be awake in someone else's dream. And so, you must do in the end what you can do from the start: confess your life and live your dream.

Are you convinced all of this is beyond your control?

Who are you, really? Look to your heart and ask if you are really life's victim. Is there no small spark of hope, of fire, that braces against such a possibility? Have you been so thoroughly trained to the idea of servitude and acquiescence in a life and world that impoverishes us all, that there is no longer even a glimmer of what might be?

Who are you, really? Are you life's victim, or have you volunteered for the role of victim in a dream from which you have been told (and have always presumed) there is no escape? What would you dream if your dream could come true? How big dare you dream?

Who are you, really—the dreamer or the dream? Are you dreaming now, or being dreamed?

## Living a Mythic Life

When your life and your dream are one, life stops being ordinary and becomes mythic. Your ordinary life becomes a sacred journey in all realms. The theater of your life becomes sacred theater. Your life ceases to be merely and only personal. People stop being personalities and become mythic figures, archetypes. You, your world, and others, express the mythos of your dream. A mythic life is lived on a very large scale. When personality is overcome, what is lived is not personal tendencies, habits, karma, but universal creative themes and possibilities: myths.

Living your dream does not mean dedicating your life to some merely personal goal. Neither does it mean living your life on some grand scale. Living your dream means living your true life purpose, manifesting love in a specific way that is personally authentic. Such a dream is never personal. We are in truth mythic beings struggling to free ourselves from the illusion that life is just a personal dilemma. Free from the illusion of personal insignificance, we discover we are beings without boundaries, with creative powers that are the stuff of myths and dreams.

## Sacred Theater

As soon as you choose to live your dream, your path of inner transformation is immediately externalized, made literal. Your dream forms the context for your inner and outer life, and the world. All things become part of your dream, part of the journey to make your dream come true. Thus, right from the start, life is a mythic journey, the world is sacred ground. The ordinary is transformed. When people interact within a dream, they generate and sustain the transforming mythic play called sacred theater.

So, your personal inner journey of enchantment becomes shared. Evolution occurs around you, not just within you. In a group, each person's dream is part of the group dream or myth. Each person plays a role in the sacred theater that is the group culture. The sacred is manifested.

Sacred theater is qualitatively different from ordinary life because it is inherently freeing and healing. Your dream naturally integrates the healing power of Roar with all other realms. Life is free, creative, and healing when you live in all realms. Group dreaming intensifies the objectivity and healing power of the dream. As you adapt to the group dream, which empowers your own, you evolve quickly. Sacred theater is a much more powerful path than a merely personal internal path. This might seem like socialization, an effort to enforce social orthodoxy. But each person participates in the collective dream having arrived independently, by his or her own dream.

Sacred theater, then, is mythic realm play in the physical realm. When someone whose life is personal interacts with someone whose life is mythic, the results can be transforming for both. The enchanter's game, group sacred theater, then becomes a means of personal evolution.

But the precondition for sacred theater is the capacity to confess, to sustain sufficient honesty and trust to make confession part of every interaction. Sacred theater is interaction without resort to the masks we use to hide from our selves and each other. Instead, we resort to masks and roles that reveal our innermost dream. Rooted in mutual honesty, the aim of sacred theater is the joy of mutual learning, healing, and creative play. Sacred theater is the game of mutual evolution. It only requires that you relax and trust the power of your dream.

Sacred theater is spontaneous, creative, interactive, intuitive theater. The learning and healing power of sacred theater is that your dream is externalized, literalized, lived right from the start. The distance between the ordinary and the sacred is zero. In sacred theater, you are invited into a fully manifested mythic play from the very beginning, not at the end of a long life journey. Evolutionary learning and healing is immediate, efficient, effective in sacred theater. You are an enchanter in an enchanted land. You transform your life and world by healing them, by living your dream of love.

All spiritual traditions, and the promise of all such traditions, are summarized and extended, redefined and reorganized in the enchanter's game.

When evolutionary learning and healing is self-induced, intuitively self-directed sacred theater, life is transformed from work into mythic play. Life stops being an ordeal and becomes a game, an adventure of mythic proportions.

Life is a story that unfolds as we dream it. It is spontaneous, interactive play—theater, organized by mutual consent and purpose, rooted in a shared dream (love), lived in a land where all dreams come true, where all dreams merge and become part of the sacred theater of an ordinary infinite life. None of this is new. What is new is that all of this is an easier and more natural process than any of us dared to hope or dream. The highest form of human life is now available to anyone willing to confess their life and live their dream.

We all have memories of sitting by a campfire, telling stories, listening to great and mythic adventures. We all remember the power of such stories. Now it is possible and time to live our dream, in love, as our expression of love. It is possible to decide how we are to live and for what purpose, not merely alone, but with others.

The ultimate outcome of creation is pro-creation, proactive creation, personal and collective creativity, love made manifest. This is our work, our life, our dream, our purpose, our destiny.

Life is a dream. What dream are you living? Whose dream are you living?

## You Are the Enchanter

So, confess your life, live your dream. If you cannot live your dream or do not know it, then confess your life, your true condition, until you are utterly empty of it. The dream will then pour out of you and you will know and live it. When you confess your life, your life changes. When you live your dream, the world changes.

You are in truth an enchanter. You are already unknowingly playing the enchanter's game. A game I created for your sake. You are a magician with powers beyond all but your dream. The way to the enchantment of life on earth demands only that you hold your dream, and let its power change your life and world. Confess these things fully and honestly, hiding nothing, hiding from nothing, until there is only love. Then, with the help of others, create the world of your dream, the world of our dreams, a life that only a dream can see.

## When Fantasy Is Reality: A Caveat

The enchanter's game has a strong attraction for those whose lives teeter on the brink of dysfunction or mediocrity. The art of dreaming calls to those who would abandon the travails of their ordinary and often unsuccessful lives for the hope of something better. That is all to the good, but those who feel called to dream often do not succeed. And therein is the caveat.

We all like the idea of dreaming. We all want lives of meaning and purpose, where we are successful and appreciated, where life is not trivialized by the constant din of merely personal needs and activities. The enchanter's art may seem like something at which you cannot fail. Everyone can dream, after all. You may think that all would be well in your life if only you could live among those who dream of life as you do. But it is not that easy.

The Enchanter's Game offers no consolations, nor respite from a hard life. It is about wisdom, power, and creativity—qualities we would all have for ourselves certainly. But such a life is not less demanding than the life you now live. It is more demanding, for you must bring those qualities to life in your self and then share them with others. Enchanters are heroes in a mythic adventure. Such a life is not for the timid or weak. There are risks that are very real. You must confront demons and darkness, fears and failure, obstacles and trials, all without warning or preparation. All these will test your powers and resolve beyond your limits.

Not the least of the many risks in this game is the madness that follows a will to confront but not to conquer your fears. The adventure of the enchanter's game results from putting yourself at risk of death—repeatedly; doing battle with your fears, again and again; always risking the possibility of losing the battle to your fears, and so becoming lost in them.

When fantasy is reality, when reality is a fantasy consciously imagined, who is to say, how are we to know, where are we to draw the line between functional creativity and madness? The enchanter's game is the sacred theater of playing god with your inner life and physical reality. You can easily become lost in a psychological labyrinth of your own making—and never know it. Playful illusion can quickly become unfortunate delusion, where all you hear is the endless echo of your own uncertainty.

The enchanter's game is best played by those willing to embrace and solve (not escape from) the problems of ordinary life in every realm. It is for those willing to risk

- madness for the sake of genius,
- mediocrity for the sake of the miraculous, and

- failure for the sake of personal and global leadership.

# The Challenge

The time is right for leaders, not teachers. We need leaders without follow-ers, who have only companions on the journey of enchantment. Such lead-ers have no tradition, provide no teachings, offer only love. The future of life on earth depends on love and all that implies. Is there any doubt of that? How, then, do we proceed to the enchantment of life on earth?

Who are you, and why are you here, really? Are you out of sync with the rest of the world? Do you seek something more in your self and the world? Do you question the meaning and purpose of your life? Are you creative, ambitious? Perhaps you need a bigger challenge in life. Consider the impos-sible. There is a world to dream, to heal, to reinvent. How can that happen until you take responsibility for the quality of life on earth, globally? It is our human destiny, an evolutionary imperative, an impossible dream. I know. The challenge is breathtaking in its scope, but is there a worthier quest, a more inspiring dream?

Do you have the time, the heart, the will, to do the impossible?

Your life can be exquisite, even glorious. Our lives can be filled with beauty, wonder, awe, adventure, excitement, peace, and compassion. It is a life you probably think is impossible. But we must not settle for suffering and struggling as the norm. Our lives need not be sad dramas clouded by dysfunction and pathology, failure and illness. The world as you now experi-ence it need not be so. Life is not a given. It is a choice.

It is time for a global renaissance rooted in personal and collective evolutionary intelligence, expressing itself as the enchantment of life on earth, the creative expression of love. Are you rebellious enough to ignore what is impossible and disciplined enough to make it practical? It is time for open-minded, good-hearted people of courage, insight, and endurance to inherit and enchant the earth. This is a challenge best suited to those with a deep passion to heal, reinvent, even transform themselves and their world. It is for those not content to watch others create the world they live in, who are serious about, and able to make and maintain a commitment to, per-sonal and global change. It is for those who know and can abide by the rules of life, but who want a better set of rules, who want to live life on a grander scale, more creatively than rules allow. It is for the warriors among us, those who want to live every moment in joyful enthusiasm, ready and eager for the challenge of life. It is for those willing to believe the impossible in order to achieve it. It is not for the timid or fainthearted.

## The Coming Storm of Intelligence

Life is demanding that we live more intelligently or perish in a wasteland of our own making. Love is the natural intelligence of life. Our dreams are its natural expression. If we are to survive our present evolutionary crisis, we must evolve to a higher level of life-affirming intelligence. Our ancient and original self asserts itself in a self-induced yet spontaneous expansion of awareness that connects us to the whole of life in all realms. This is the higher level of life-affirming intelligence. It is love. We must evolve into a new way of being human, a new kind of human being possible only when we live our dreams in love.

Evolution is the reorganization of intelligence. Problems that appear, but cannot be solved, at one evolutionary level are internalized and easily solved at the next higher level of evolutionary intelligence. This is the nature and the possibility of enchantment.

Imagine how your life would evolve if you suddenly were more intelligent—not more knowledgeable, but more creative, intuitive, insightful, loving. Every aspect of your life would function at a higher level. You would live on a grander scale. Wisdom, freedom, joy, mental and emotional health, kindness, environmental harmony, power, and community would typify your life. The paradigm of human life would shift from competition to cooperation. Your life would be enchanted. When the mind falls into the heart, and the heart falls to earth, love and intelligence converge. There is the enchantment of life on earth.

Evolution is here as a storm of intelligence already putting our lives and world into disarray. But this only clears the way for what must follow: a new and higher order of human life lived on a global scale. Enchantment is the force of life overcoming the limits we impose on it. When the dust settles, we will see that the storm was not the chaos of change waiting for us to impose order, but the emergence of a new and higher order of human intelligence itself.

As human beings, we are naturally inclined to the enchantments of love. So is our world. We can reclaim our lost and ancient powers to heal and creatively express love in the world. The way to this enchantment of life on earth is contained in a single and simple strategy: a relentless intent to dream a world in love.

What are you willing to risk to live your dream of love?

Is this fantasy . . . or fact?
You are the judge. I am the witness.
What is your judgment?
There is an initiation, a doorway, a threshold, a line.
This is the line. Will you cross it?

# About the Author

EDWIN SMITH HAS STUDIED AND PRACTICED within a variety of spiritual traditions and schools of psychology. He holds an M.S. degree in psychology with empasis in counseling and organizational development. He is the author of *Do You See What I See?*

Smith has lived in the Pacific Northwest for over twenty-five years. He works with individuals or groups who have a sincere interest in personal enlightenment or global transformation. You can reach Ed at his website, *www.relentlesslove.com*.

Sentient Publications, LLC publishes books on cultural creativity, experimental education, transformative spirituality, holistic health, new science, and ecology, approached from an integral viewpoint. Our authors are intensely interested in exploring the nature of life from fresh perspectives, addressing life's great questions, and fostering the full expression of the human potential. Sentient Publications' books arise from the spirit of inquiry and the richness of the inherent dialogue between writer and reader.

We are very interested in hearing from our readers. To direct suggestions or comments to us, or to be added to our mailing list, please contact:

### SENTIENT PUBLICATIONS, LLC
1113 Spruce Street
Boulder, CO 80302
303.443.2188
contact@sentientpublications.com
www.sentientpublications.com